Why was Queen Victoria Such A Prude?

...and other historical myths and follies

DAVID HAVILAND

ISBN-13: 978-1909609013
ISBN-10:1909609013

CONTENTS

1

BYGONE BLUNDERS

'History teaches us that men and nations behave wisely once
they have exhausted all other alternatives.'

Abba Eban (1915-2002)

What was the most disastrous kidnapping in history?

The answer to this question is surely the kidnapping of
Sparta's Queen Helen by the Trojan prince Paris, which
led to the disastrous Trojan War. Until very recently, the stories
of Troy in Greek literature had been thought to have been purely
mythical, until archaeological evidence appeared in the late 20th
century which seemed to confirm that Troy had indeed existed,
and had been a major strategic city of the time, which had undergone a number of lengthy conflicts some time around the 12th or
13th century BC. Based on this evidence, it seems likely that the
stories told in the classical Greek literature, particularly Homer's
Odyssey and *The Iliad*, were based to some extent on genuine historical events, although these seem to have been combined with
existing myths and legends.

According to these sources, the Trojan War was sparked by the kidnapping of Helen by Paris, prince of Troy. Helen was the wife of Meneleus, King of Sparta, and she was renowned as being the most beautiful woman in the world, famously described by Goethe many centuries later as 'the face that launched a thousand ships'. The abduction of Helen led to a ten-year military campaign, in which the Greek forces led by Agamemnon took control of Troy's allies and neighbours, and laid siege to the walled city of Troy itself. However, Troy seemed to be impenetrable.

In the tenth year, Troy at last fell, thanks to a brilliant scheme devised by Odysseus, which has come to be known as the Trojan Horse. The plan went as follows. First, the Greek forces burned down their camp and left, leaving behind an enormous horse made of wood. Attached to this horse was a note, which explained that the horse was a ceremonial gift to the Trojans, in recognition of their victory. Clearly, it seemed, the Greeks had admitted defeat, and sailed home. The Trojans opened the gates of the city, dragged the enormous horse inside, and began a night of boozy celebrations.

Later that same night, once all the Trojans were drunk or asleep, a group of 30 Greek soldiers emerged from inside the wooden horse. They then opened the gates of the city, to let in the rest of the Greek army, which had sailed silently back to Troy under cover of night. The Greek army now attacked, razing the city to the ground, massacring the male population, and emphatically ending the war.

Why didn't the Vikings settle in North America?
For centuries it was thought that the first European discovery of the Americas took place in 1492, with the arrival of Christopher Columbus, but the continent had in fact been

discovered almost 500 years earlier, by the all conquering Vikings, some time around the year 1000. The Vikings were the world's leading sea power at this time, and they were hungry for land in which to continue their expansion. They had already colonised Iceland in the late 9th century, and then Greenland in around 980. Iceland is around 1,000 miles west of Norway, and then Greenland is a further 700 miles west of Iceland. Newfoundland in Canada is only another 600 miles from Greenland, and it's even possible that cloud formations coming off the mountains of Baffin Island may have been visible from the coastal mountains of Greenland. It's therefore no surprise that the Vikings soon became aware of the new land to the west, and it wasn't long before they had begun to explore it.

Greenland had been settled by the dangerous outlaw Erik the Red, who had been banished from Iceland for committing a number of murders, as a result of a bizarre dispute over the ownership of some ornamented wooden beams (beams which, in all probability, Erik had simply stolen from the eventual murder victims). The 'red' of Erik's name may have been a reference to the colour of his hair, or more likely his blood-soaked reputation. The exiled Erik thus settled in Greenland, and when he returned temporarily to Iceland, he came telling stories of a lush, fertile land, which he disingenuously named 'Greenland', in order to lure settlers to join him in the new colony. In fact, of course, Greenland is almost entirely covered with ice, the whole year round. Erik explained the deception, 'People would be more eager to go there if the land had a good name.' His plan succeeded, and Erik was soon in charge of two settlements in Greenland.

Leif Ericson was one of Erik the Red's sons, and in some time around the year 1002-3 he set out on a voyage west, in the hope of discovering new lands. He made a number of landings, the first of which he named 'Helluland', which means 'land of flat rocks'; this may have been Baffin Island. He next reached 'Markland', meaning 'wood-land', which may have been Labrador. He then made landfall at a place he called 'Vinland', in reference to the abundant grapes he found growing there. Ericson established a settlement on Vinland, and in the spring he travelled back to Greenland with a cargo of timber. Over the next few years, the colony began to grow, despite occasional battles with the native, pre-Inuit population.

The story of the Vinland settlement appears in the Norse Sagas of the 13th and 14th centuries, and there is also compelling archaeological evidence for the existence of the colony. Archaeologists have found the remains of a Viking settlement at L'Anse aux Meadows, at the northernmost tip of Newfoundland in Canada. This small Viking village consists of 8 buildings, including an iron smithy, a carpentry workshop, and a boatyard. A number of recognisably Norse items have been found at the site, including an oil lamp, a needle, and a fastening pin, and carbon dating has established the site at around the year 1000. Furthermore, the archaeological evidence confirms the story told in the Norse Sagas that Vinland was only briefly inhabited, before being abandoned, which raises the question: why did the Vikings leave? Newfoundland has a much more pleasant and fertile climate than Iceland or Greenland; it is not much further west, relatively speaking; and the Norsemen were hungry for new land. So what happened to prevent the Vikings from permanently settling in North America?

Amazingly, the answer seems to come down to a relatively trivial family dispute, involving Leif Ericson's half-sister, Freydís Eiríksdóttir. Freydís appears to have a fearsome woman. In one story which has survived, we are told that she witnessed a group of Norse settlers retreating while being chased by angry natives. At this, she taunted the Vikings for their cowardice, and demanded they give her a weapon, claiming that she would show them how to fight, despite the fact that she was pregnant at the time. She then bared one of her breasts, and hacked at it with her sword. This extraordinary display is said to have terrified the natives, who quickly fled.

Freydis had sailed to Vinland with two business partners, Helgi and Finnbogi, with whom she had promised to split the profits of their enterprise. However, after a time she changed her mind, and had the pair killed. Then, she insisted that their wives and children should all be killed too, but even her own brutal followers drew the line at such an atrocity, and refused to take part, so she simply went ahead and murdered the women and children herself. When the story of this outrage reached Greenland, there was a public scandal, particularly as Leif Ericson refused to have Freydís executed, even though this was the mandatory punishment, because of his affection for her as a brother. To avoid any further scandals, Ericson banned all Vikings from travelling to Vinland, as the settlement didn't seem to be worth the trouble. This prohibition was respected for decades, even after Ericson's death, and as a result the colony was never revived, and an entire continent was lost.

How did an inaccurate oil painting cost Thomas Cromwell his life?

Thomas Cromwell enjoyed an extraordinary rise from humble beginnings. He was born in 1485, to a father who worked as a blacksmith, fuller, and clothworker, and yet by 1523 Thomas Cromwell had become a Member of Parliament, and nine years later he was King Henry VIII's chief minister, with unprecedented power over every aspect of both secular life and the Church. Cromwell was a key figure in pushing through the English Reformation, in which Henry VIII broke off all ties with the Roman Catholic Church and made himself the Supreme Head of the Church of England. Cromwell presided over the dissolution of the monasteries, and as a result became deeply unpopular, particularly among the clergy.

The Reformation was instigated by Henry's desire to have his marriage to Catherine of Aragon annulled, on the grounds that she had been married to his older brother Arthur. The real reason was so that he could marry the young, attractive Anne Boleyn, who might be able to succeed where the older Catherine had sadly failed in producing a male heir (Catherine had given birth to two boys, but both had died in infancy). However, the subsequent marriage to Anne also failed to produce a male heir, and so in 1536 she was executed, on charges of adultery, incest, and treason, which were almost certainly trumped up. The day after Anne's execution, Henry became engaged to Jane Seymour, one of Anne's ladies-in-waiting, and within ten days they were married. The following year, Jane gave birth to a son, Edward, but died of complications following the birth.

Three years later, Henry was again keen to marry, in the hope of securing his succession by producing a second heir. Understandably, however, the noblewomen of Europe were not exactly queuing up to become Henry's fourth wife, given what had happened to the first three. Cromwell pushed for Henry to marry Anne of Cleves, the sister of the Protestant Duke of Cleves, in the hope that this political match would secure Henry the support of the northern German princes, in case of an attack from the Franco-Habsburg Catholic powers. Henry had never seen or met Anne, so he sent the artist Hans Holbein to Cleves to paint portraits of her and her younger sister (both of whom Henry was considering), and specifically instructed Holbein to make the pictures accurate, rather than flattering. When Holbein returned with the completed portraits, Henry found that Anne was to his liking, and so the marriage treaty was arranged.

Anne now travelled to England, but her first meeting with Henry was not a success. Reportedly, when he entered the room at Greenwich Palace, she did not recognise him, and so she simply ignored him, and carried on gazing out of the window. Anne was uneducated, and did not speak any English; and Henry found her physically unattractive. He had brought a hamper of New Year's gifts to Greenwich to give to Anne, but decided against it, and kept them for himself. He later raged at Cromwell, feeling he had been tricked into the arrangement for the sake of his minister's preferred political alliance. He complained to Cromwell that Holbein's portrait had been inaccurate: 'I see no such thing in her as hath been showed me. I like her not,' and dubbed her the 'Flanders Mare'. He demanded that Cromwell get him out of the marriage treaty, but Cromwell insisted that by this point it was just too late, and so the wedding went ahead. That night, the marriage went unconsummated, as Henry could only bring himself to give Anne a light kiss on the forehead, before retiring to his own bedroom. He commented after the wedding, 'I liked her before not well, but now I like her much worse.'

Henry swiftly made plans to annul the marriage, and Anne was wise enough to agree to them, no doubt aware of the other possible outcomes. As a result, Henry looked on her with affection for the rest of his life, describing her as 'the King's Beloved Sister', and giving her properties including Richmond Palace and Hever Castle. After Henry's next marriage to Catherine Howard failed, Anne and Henry were on such good terms that she even suggested he remarry her (despite the fact that Catherine Howard had just become the second of Henry's wives to be beheaded), but Henry firmly declined.

Anne may have eventually found herself in the King's good graces, but for Cromwell the situation was far more grave. After the wedding, he was banished from Henry's court, and cut off from royal support. This was the opportunity Cromwell's many enemies had been waiting for, and they were quick to strike. On 10 June, 1540, Cromwell was arrested and imprisoned in the Tower of London, and subjected to an Act of Attainder. On 28 July, he was executed on Tower Hill, on the same day that Henry was married to Catherine Howard. Cromwell's head was then boiled, and displayed on a spike on London Bridge, facing away from the City.

What was the worst apology in history?

The 'non-apology apology' has become a depressing feature of modern political life, a deliberately hollow form of words that attempts to sound like an apology, without any actual admission of guilt or wrongdoing. When, for example, President George H. W. Bush's chief of staff John H. Sununu was caught breaking White House travel rules in 1991, he issued a slippery statement: 'Clearly, no one regrets more than I do the appearance of impropriety. Obviously, some mistakes were made.' Six years later, President Clinton offered a similarly empty apology, after inviting banking officials to a meeting of Democrat fundraisers: 'Mistakes were made here by people who either did it deliberately or inadvertently.'

However, when it comes to historical non-apology apologies, few can match that issued by the stern, uncompromising Scottish clergyman John Knox to Queen Elizabeth in 1558. Knox was a leading Protestant reformer, whose life would have been significantly easier had it not been for the existence of three women named Mary. In 1546, Knox had been exiled from Scotland by the Catholic Regent, Mary of Guise. Furthermore, there seemed little hope of Scotland turning to Protestantism even if Mary of Guise where removed, as the heir apparent was her Catholic daughter, Mary Stuart, who would go on to become Mary Queen of Scots. In England, Knox's star had risen under King Edward VI, as he reached the position of Royal Chaplain, but when the young king died in 1553, he was succeeded by his sister, Mary Tudor, who returned England to Catholicism, and Knox found himself banished once again.

In response to these setbacks, in 1558 Knox issued an anonymous, provocative pamphlet called 'The First Blast of the Trumpet Against the Monstrous Regimen of Women'. In it, he raged against what he felt to be an absurd situation in which so much power was in the hands of women, in what was clearly a disruption of the natural order. He wrote, 'It is more than a monster in nature that a woman should reign and bear empire over man.' The pamphlet was highly controversial, and it did nothing to further Knox's cause, particularly when later that year Mary Tudor was succeeded by her Protestant sister, Elizabeth, who could potentially have been a great ally to Knox.

Knox held Elizabeth in high regard, and hoped that she might allow him to return from exile, and perhaps even take up a bishopric. However, Elizabeth had been infuriated by the pamphlet, and made it clear that Knox's name was not even to be spoken in her presence. Knox now attempted to apologise, writing a personal letter to the Queen, but his apology may be said to have left something to be desired. 'I cannot deny the writing of a book against the usurped authority and unjust government of women,' he wrote, 'neither yet am I minded to recant or call back any principal point or proposition of the same, till truth and verity do further appear.' Surely, he went on, Elizabeth could recognise that she was only in power by 'a peculiar dispensation of God's mercy, permitting in her what law and nature denied to all other women.' In short, he essentially insisted that he had been right all along about the role of women, and that Elizabeth must surely have known it, and agreed with him. If, however, she would humbly submit to God, he explained that he could be prepared to find it within himself to tolerate her reign.

Amazingly, Elizabeth wasn't won over by this unusual approach to the billet-doux, and so while other Protestant exiles were welcomed back to the fold, Knox remained persona non grata. In 1560, he would play a central role in the Scottish Reformation, but even then he was excluded from any negotiations with England, as his presence was deemed to be just too offensive to Elizabeth to be tolerated, and she never forgave him.

Did a chauffeur's wrong turn lead to World War One?

On 28 June 1914, the heir to the Austro-Hungarian throne Archduke Franz Ferdinand was shot dead in Sarajevo by the Serbian Gavrilo Princep, a member of the Black Hand terrorist organisation. In 1907, Bosnia and Herzegovina had been subsumed into Austria-Hungary, but these provinces contained a significant population of ethnic Serbs and Slavs, and so Serbian nationalists were keen to see them break away from Austria-Hungary, and form part of a Greater Serbia. The Black Hand sought to achieve this goal through terrorist attacks, and made plans to assassinate a number of leading Austro-Hungarian figures. When an attempt on the Governor of Bosnia, Oskar Potiorek, was called off, Archduke Franz Ferdinand became the new target.

The assassination was set to take place on the 28th June, a date loaded with significance for Serbs, as it is a patriotic public holiday which commemorates the Battle of Kosovo against the Ottoman Turks in 1389. On the day itself, the conspiracy collapsed in a series of blunders. Six assassins were positioned along the route of Ferdinand's motorcade, but as the cars passed, the first two assassins did nothing, presumably because they lost their nerve. The third assassin, Nedeljko Čabrinović, did throw a bomb at Ferdinand's car, but missed, and instead blew up the next car in the motorcade, wounding about twenty people in the process. As the crowd panicked, Čabrinović quickly swallowed his suicide pill, and jumped into the River Miljacka, but the river was only a few inches deep, and the pill only succeeded in making him vomit. He was dragged out of the 'river', and severely beaten by the crowd, before being led away by police, while supposedly shouting, 'I am a Serbian hero.'

Amazingly, despite the attack, the Archduke decided to continue with his visit. He attended a town hall reception, where he interrupted Mayor Curcic to complain, 'Mr Mayor, I came here on a visit and I get bombs thrown at me. It is outrageous.' After leaving the town hall, the motorcade then headed for the hospital, to visit those wounded by the bomb. On the way, the cars took a wrong turn, and so Ferdinand's driver reversed into an alley, to turn around. There, the car happened by chance to pull up alongside one of the terrorists,

Gavrilo Princip, who was himself in the wrong place, having been given faulty directions. Spotting his opportunity, Princep quickly fired his pistol into the car, killing both Ferdinand and his wife, Sophie.

One mysterious aspect of this story is why Franz Ferdinand chose to go to Sarajevo in the first place. The Austro-Hungarian government had received a number of specific warnings that Franz Ferdinand was being targeted for assassination, but he still went ahead with a trip which was unquestionably provocative, dangerous, and pretty much pointless. Then, he chose to ride around the streets of Sarajevo in an open-topped car with the roof down. Amazingly, even after a bomb had hit the convoy, Ferdinand persisted with the visit, and seems to have taken no additional precautions; for example, he remained in the open-topped car, rather than switching vehicles.

The assassination of Franz Ferdinand was the trigger for the outbreak of the First World War One, which began just one month later. One might therefore argue that if Franz Ferdinand's chauffeur hadn't reversed down that alley, the assassination may never have taken place, and the bloodiest war the world had ever seen might have been averted. However, the chauffeur's wrong turn was only one tiny factor in the events that unfolded. The assassins had many opportunities to kill the Archduke that day, and if Princep hadn't been standing on that particular street corner, there's no reason to think the killing wouldn't have taken place on a different street. And if the Black Hand had failed to kill Ferdinand, it seems likely that they would have succeeded with a different target soon enough.

Of course, the assassination of Franz Ferdinand was only the spark which ignited the European powder-keg. After the bloodshed and destruction of the Napoleonic Wars, the major European powers had agreed in 1815 to pursue a policy based on 'balance of power', whereby the nations would form powerful alliances so that no one nation or block would become dominant, and so war would be averted. The policy was largely successful for a century, but when Kaiser Wilhelm II ascended to the throne, he was eager for Germany to build a global empire of her own, to match those of Britain, France, Belgium and Holland. Germany's aggressive international approach included offering an 'open-hand' policy offering unequivocal support for Austria-Hungary. After the assassination, Austria-Hungary declared war on Serbia, with Russia immediately supporting Serbia, and Germany backing Austria. France joined Russia, followed by Britain, in response to Germany's advance through Belgium, and so the Great War had begun.

Which is the more effective weapon: a bayonet, or a machine gun?

The answer may seem obvious, but for decades this question was the source of considerable debate among serious-minded military experts. The first viable machine guns had been available since the 1860s, but even as late as World War One, Britain's military strategists felt that machine guns were overrated and unwieldy, and could be defeated by aggressive bayonet charges, despite the mounting evidence to the contrary. Only after more than a million men had died in the Great War did this orthodoxy start to change.

In fairness, the effectiveness of machine guns was not quite as obvious as it may seem in hindsight. Bayonet charges had proved to be consistently effective since the 17th century. Napoleon's Imperial Guard had famously inspired terror with their bayonet charges, and the weapon was widely believed to instil aggression in the attacking forces, while wreaking fear among the defenders. Bayonets are cheap to produce, easy to maintain, require no ammunition, and pose little risk to your comrades in close quarter fighting, unlike bullets.

Machine guns on the other hand seemed to be riddled with flaws. They were expensive and used up too much ammunition. They could easily get jammed, and they were difficult to repair. They were heavy, and couldn't be easily moved, so they were useless for mobile warfare. As such, it was thought that machine guns could only be useful as a defensive weapon, whereas everyone knew that historically wars were won by aggressive, offensive strategy. Britain's generals thus failed to anticipate the advent of trench warfare, even though many recent conflicts had involved entrenched fighting, including the Russo-Japanese War (1904-5), the Second Boer War (1899-1902), and even as far back as the US Civil War (1861-1865). In fact, the lesson that had been taken from the Russo-Japanese War was that the Russians' machine guns had not been decisive, because Japan had won. However, this assessment failed to appreciate the huge losses suffered by the Japanese.

As the Great War progressed, it ought to have quickly become clear that Britain's slow, orderly advances into barbed wire and machine gun fire did not constitute a winning strategy. Tommies joked that their bayonets were more useful for chopping wood and opening cans than they were for combat. At Neuve Chapelle, the first major bayonet charge of 1915 resulted in 90 percent casualties for the Allies. In September of the same year, at the Battle of Loos, 80 percent of the British attacking force were killed or wounded, while the Germans were largely unscathed.

Even so, a year later, Field Marshal Sir Douglas Haig still felt confident reporting to the War Office that, 'the machine gun is a much overrated weapon, two per battalion is more than sufficient.' The war, felt Haig, would be won by cavalry because, 'Bullets have little stopping-power against the horse.' At the First Battle of the Somme in 1916, many battalion commanders chose to ignore or 'misunderstand' the ordered bayonet charge, which the British Expeditionary Force commanders specifically stated must take place at a walking pace. By 1917, the tactic was gradually being phased out, with every company being issued with at least four Lewis light machine guns. At the end of the war, it was estimated that only 0.3 percent of enemy casualties had been inflicted by bayonets.

What was the flaw in the Maginot Line?
After World War One, France was determined to never again suffer such a dreadful cost in terms of human lives, buildings, and infrastructure. However, after the punitive settlement at the Treaty of Versailles, it seemed likely that Germany would seek revenge, and so France needed to plan her defence. A number of options were considered, but the chosen plan was a vast, permanent fortification that would protect the whole of France's border with Germany, from the Swiss border all the way up to the Ardennes. It became known as the Maginot Line, after the French Minister of War André Maginot, who oversaw the project, and died during its construction.

Despite the name, the Maginot Line was not a single fortification, but rather a series of forts, at intervals of around nine miles. In some areas, the Line simply comprised the natural geography, where mountains or rivers made the border impassable. The biggest forts, called 'ouvrages', housed 1,000 soldiers with artillery, and these were supported by smaller, intermediate forts with around 200-500 men in each. The Maginot Line was also a much wider zone than its name suggests, being up to 25 kilometres wide in parts, consisting of a system of fortifications, guard posts, communication centres, barricades, artillery, anti-tank gun emplacements, supply depots, as well as barracks, hospitals, powerlines, ammunition dumps, and a narrow-gauge railway line.

The Maginot Line was widely admired, and visited by military strategists from around the world. Czechoslovakia built its own Maginot Line, based largely on the French plans. The French Maginot Line was intended to slow any German advance, prevent the possibility of a surprise attack, and give the French time to mobilise their forces. The line would ensure that most of the fighting took place on the France-Germany border, thus minimising damage to property and infrastructure, and if the Line was breached, the German forces would find themselves under attack from the rear, from the nearby ouvrages.

However, despite its theoretical merits, the Maginot Line turned out to have a significant flaw: to put it simply, it wasn't finished. The Line ran from the Swiss border up to the Ardennes forest, at the junction of the borders of France, Belgium, and Luxembourg. However, the Line stopped here, and did not cover the France-Belgium border, because the Belgians, who were determined to remain neutral, stated that they would see this as an act of aggression. As a result, when Germany inevitably invaded Belgium in May 1940, the Allies found themselves fighting along a largely unprotected border. When the Germans then surged through the Ardennes, the Allied forces were cut in half, and hundreds of thousands had to be evacuated from Dunkirk. Meanwhile the Luftwaffe simply flew over the Maginot Line. Within weeks, Paris had fallen, and France was calling for an Armistice. The Maginot

Line remained intact; pristine but irrelevant, as the French ordered their troops to come out of the fortifications, to be assembled as prisoners of war.

What was the Groundnut Army?

In 1946, the British government launched an ambitious plan to grow peanuts in the African protectorate of Tanganyika, which is today known as Tanzania. The plan was proposed by Frank Samuel of Unilever, who felt peanuts, which are also known as groundnuts, could provide a useful source of oils and fats, both of which were in short supply. The government authorised a budget of £25 million, with the aim of cultivating 150,000 acres of scrubland in six years. A site was selected in central Tanganyika, and 100,000 ex-soldiers were recruited to form the 'Groundnut Army', with a mission to fatten up Britain after the privations of years of rationing.

The project was launched in an optimistic spirit of British can-do, but there were soon signs that pluck and muddling through might not be enough. The first job was to clear the land, and the preliminary planning report had simply assumed that local machinery would be used, but in fact there was no suitable machinery, either in Tanganyika or anywhere else. There were no heavy-duty tractors in Britain, and those nations which did have this type of heavy machinery were already using it, to rebuild their own countries after the war. Eventually, some available tractors were found in Canada, as well as hundreds of old American bulldozers which had been left behind in the Phillipines, and were intended for disposal.

Once the machinery had been freighted to the port at Dar-es-Salaam, the question was how to get it to the groundnut site at Kongwa. The port had no deep-water berths to allow the freighters to come into the dock, and so makeshift arrangements had to be made to lift the heavy equipment from the ships onto the quay. The quayside was soon piled high with great quantities of equipment and provisions, but the next problem was how to transport it all to the site. There were no suitable roads, and only one solitary rail line, from the port to Kongwa, and this was soon washed away by a flood. Nonetheless, the brave pioneers persevered along the inadequate road, frequently beset by charging elephants, packs of aggressive baboons, and lions leaping on the back of their trucks. Eventually, in the face of every imaginable obstacle, the party arrived at Kongwa.

The next challenge was to clear the earth, but this too was much harder than had been foreseen. According to one report, the scrub was so thick that although a rhinoceros could charge through it, and a snake could wriggle its way through, no creature of any size in between could possibly hope to get through. Tractors were not up to the job, but eventually pairs of bulldozers were found to be able to make some progress, although the roots tended to wear out the blades of the bulldozers within a matter of days. There was also the problem of enormous baobab trees, some of which were over twenty feet in diameter. Not only were these extremely tough to clear, they often contained hives of extremely aggressive local bees. One tree was found to contain two natives; it was being used as a tribal jail. The British also managed to upset the local African population when a tree containing an old skull was toppled – it seemed that the skull had belonged to a revered figure, the 'Unknown One', and so the Groundnut Army had caused a grave insult.

As the project struggled on, the administrators decided to make more use of local African workers, but this too was fraught with problems. Locals were employed to drive the tractors, but their enthusiasm and inexperience meant many machines were crashed and ruined. The Colonial Office in London encouraged the native workers to form a trade union, being keen to encourage proper working practices, but within days the newly unionised workers had gone on strike, armed themselves, and formed a roadblock between Kongwa and the port.

The project also had a number of damaging indirect effects on the local community. The arrival of the Ground-nut Army caused dramatic price inflation, and soon food had become too expensive for many of the tribespeople, and many babies died of malnutrition. As the local African tribes grew to depend on the Groundnut Army for work and money, respect for traditional tribal leaders declined, and so the foundations of the local society were undermined. Local women turned to prostitution, but soon found they were competing with professional sex workers, who moved to the area in significant numbers.

Even once the ground had been cultivated, there were still significant problems, as the Tanganyikan soil and climate were simply not suitable for growing groundnuts. There was no local water source, so water had to be transported to the site (where it was stored in a concrete reservoir, which the locals insisted on using as a swimming pool). The local soil contained a high proportion of clay, which made it rock-hard once it had baked in the African sun. Since groundnuts grow underground, this meant that even when the Ground-nut Army did manage to grow some nuts, they were almost impossible to harvest.

In 1951, the scheme was abandoned, in one of the last acts of the outgoing Labour government. Project leader Major-General Desmond Harrison had had a nervous breakdown, and had been brought home on sick leave. Overall, the ill-fated project had cost the British taxpayer £49 million, with nothing to show in return. The project had bought 4,000 tons of groundnuts for seed, but only succeeded in growing a total of 2,000 tons of nuts, half as many as had been bought in the first place.

Ten years after the project had been abandoned, workers would occasionally find tractors buried in the land around Kongwa. It seems that, during the Groundnut project, the tractor drivers were paid by the hour, and these hours were determined by timers attached to the tractors' engines. Some of the more ingenious drivers realised that if they drove into the bush, there were depressions in the ground where the tractors could be hidden out of sight. So, they would simply leave their tractor in one of these craters, with the engine running, and go into town for the day. Later, they would come back to reclaim their machine, but sometimes they wouldn't be able to find it, and so the tractors were simply left there, gathering dust.

What was the 'Great Leap Forward'?

The Great Leap Forward was the name given to a series of economic policies instigated by the Chinese Communist government between 1958-61, which caused one of the worst economic and humanitarian disasters in history. The plan was based on the belief of Communist dictator Mao Zedong that China needed to move as rapidly as possible from an agrarian society to an industrial one, to catch up with its Western rivals.

To achieve this, a number of absurdly ambitious targets were set, with the goal of exponentially increasing China's steel production. Chairman Mao claimed that China would overtake Britain in steel production within 15 years, but a year later this target was brought forward, to a single year. This was to be achieved by increasing grain production, so that grain surpluses could be sold for export, and by creating 600,000 backyard steel furnaces throughout China. Private ownership of land was abolished, and all farms were forcibly taken over by local state-controlled collectives, with wages replaced with 'work points'.

One of the first steps was to eliminate the so-called 'Four Pests' which Mao felt were harming China's agricultural productivity. These were: flies, mosquitoes, rats, and sparrows. Only after an extended campaign of slaughter did it become clear that these creatures, sparrows in particular, played a pivotal role in the food chain, and soon crops were being decimated by locusts. Other untested farming methods and theories were introduced, such as close cropping, in which seeds were planted much more densely than normal, in the mistaken belief that they would somehow avoid competing with each other. Productive land was left fallow, so that resources could be focussed on the most fertile land, thus increasing per-acre yields, but cutting total production.

The most disastrous aspect of the Great Leap Forward was the decision to focus China's resources on the production of steel. High quality steel can only be produced in properly equipped factories with a steady supply of coal and iron ore. However, Mao knew nothing about metallurgy, and so insisted that every commune should establish its own small backyard furnaces. To meet the ambitious targets, people began melting down their pots and pans, which meant that they now had nothing to cook with. They then melted their tractors, hoes, spades, and buckets, leaving them without machinery or tools to work with. Soon, people were taking down the fences that enclosed their cattle, and taking the nails and screws out of their homes. The steel furnaces needed a continuous supply of fuel, and so hillsides and orchards were stripped of trees, leading to erosion and flooding. And the end result of all these efforts was steel of such poor quality that 99 percent of it was unusable. Instead of industrialising, China had managed the fastest programme of deindustrialisation in history, melting down all of its steel tools and machinery to produce worthless pig iron.

Chairman Mao's targets may have been unrealistic, but the commune leaders knew better than to admit that they had failed. Instead, they competed for approval by providing inflated figures, claiming that grain yields were much higher than they actually were. As a result, vast quantities of grain were taken for export, leaving the communes that had produced them starving. As Mao travelled around China, commune leaders transported the same piles of grain from one area to the next, to create the impression of surpluses.

Mao's disastrous plan caused enormous hardship and suffering. While communes were forced to devote their energies to steel production, tons of grain was left to wither in the fields, unharvested. As the madness intensified, there was no time to plant crops for next year. In one commune which had enjoyed a good harvest, 35 percent of the peasants still starved to death, because the grain was left to rot in the fields. Punishments for minor crimes and dissent became unimaginably cruel, with victims being tied up and thrown into lakes, buried alive, or set on fire. Many were forced to work naked in the middle of winter, or starved to death by being banned from the communal canteens. As China starved, there were even incidences of cannibalism, and reports of parents eating their own babies.

The consequences of this folly were devastating. Around 30-45 million people died, mostly of starvation, but also from beatings, torture, and suicide. The famine was exacerbated by poor weather conditions, with flooding and droughts in 1959 and 1960 making the famine considerably worse. By 1961, the insanity of the Great Leap Forward had become clear even to Mao, who stood down as Head of State. The steel production was halted, and grain was imported from Canada and the United States.

2

HISTORICAL MYTHS

'A little inaccuracy sometimes saves tons of explanation.'
Saki (1870-1916)

Is there any truth to the story of the Minotaur?

One of the most enduring stories of Greek mythology is that of Theseus and the Minotaur, a terrifying creature which was half man, half bull. The creature was the result of the union between Pasiphaë, the wife of King Minos of Crete, and a snow-white bull, with which she had fallen in love. The bull had been sent to Minos by Poseidon, god of the sea, to be sacrificed, but Minos instead decided to keep the beautiful bull. To punish Minos, Aphrodite made Pasiphaë fall in love with the bull. Then, in a particularly graphic detail, a wooden cow was constructed, so that Pasiphaë could climb into it, and have sex with the bull. The result of this grotesque coupling was the fearsome Minotaur, which King Minos kept trapped in an elaborate maze underneath his palace, which was known as the labyrinth.

Every year, according to the story, the people of Athens would have to pay tribute to Crete, by sending seven young men and women, who would be sent into the labyrinth, to be fed to the Minotaur. The Athenian hero Theseus however vowed to kill the beast, and travelled to Crete as part of the sacrificial party. On the night of his arrival, Minos's daughter Ariadne came to Theseus's room, having fallen in love with him, and gave him a sword and a ball of twine, to help him defeat the Minotaur.

The next day, Theseus entered the labyrinth, unraveling the ball of twine as he went, to help him retrace his steps. He confronted the Minotaur, and killed it with his sword, before finding his way out of the labyrinth using the ball of twine. He then sailed for home, along with the other young Cretans he had rescued. However, on this journey Theseus became bored of Ariadne, and so abandoned her on the island of Naxos. As a punishment, the gods made him forget the sign he had agreed with his father, King Aegeus – if Theseus had survived, he was supposed to raise a white sail, so that Aegeus would know his son was safe. When Theseus's ship appeared on the horizon, Aegeus saw only black sails raised and, thinking the worst, threw himself off a cliff.

Clearly, many elements of this story are supernatural and fantastical, but like many stores from Greek mythology, there does seem to be a historical core. Crete really was ruled by King Minos, and the ruins of his palace at Knossos have been found. The palace contains an enormous, complex network of passages, staircases, and cellars, which may be the origin of the labyrinth. During the reign of King Minos, Crete does appear to have been the most powerful city-state in the region, and so it is quite plausible that weaker neighbours would have been be required to pay tribute, and that this tribute may have included young men and women for sacrifice. Furthermore, some historians have suggested that this sacrifice could well have been performed by a priest wearing a bull's head or mask, as the bull was the symbol of Crete. Furthermore, there is also evidence that the Cretans would torture their victims by enclosing them in the belly of a red-hot metal bull, so it does seem that the story of the Minotaur may well be based on a historical practice.

When was the Great Wall of China built?

The Great Wall of China is an extraordinary feat of construction, which stretches for more than 5,500 miles. However, the question of when the wall was built is somewhat trickier than it might sound at first, as it bears comparison with the philosophical question of 'my grandfather's axe'. For those not familiar with it, this puzzling question describes an axe, passed down from the teller's grandfather, which in that time has had both its handle and its head replaced a number of times. Since none of the original parts are still physically present, to what extent can it be considered to be the same axe?

Similarly, the Great Wall of China has undergone extensive renovation, rebuilding, and remodelling, so that very little of the original Great Wall is actually in evidence. The first sections of the wall were built in the 5th century BC, when a number of China's warring states built extensive fortifications to defend their borders. When Qin Shi Huang conquered the states four centuries later in 221 BC, he established the Qin Dynasty, and became China's first Emperor. Now, having united the country, he ordered that all the internal walls between the states should be demolished. Instead, a long series of fortifications was to be built along China's northern border with Mongolia. Thus, some of the sections of wall which had been built in the 5th century BC did form part of the new external wall, but the Great Wall as a project arguably only commenced in 221 BC.

Construction of the wall was an enormous project, which took place under terrible conditions. The army of labourers was conscripted, and included dissenters and political prisoners. Around 3 million labourers and prisoners are thought to have worked on the Qin dynasty section of the wall, which covers 3,000 miles. Of those, more than a million died in the course of construction, which means there were, on average, 300 deaths for every mile of wall built.

Over the following centuries, the wall continued to be repaired, rebuilt and extended, but it wasn't until the Ming Dynasty of the 15th century that the next major phase occurred. The Ming army had lost a series of battles against the tribes of Manchuria and Mongolia, and so the Ming empire now built a new wall, along the southern edge of the Ordos Desert. Unlike the Qin Dynasty wall, which had been constructed mainly of rammed earth with some stones, the Ming wall was stronger, being made of bricks. This wall was successful in holding back the Manchu invaders, who only managed to cross it in 1644 when they were let through by a rebel border general.

Most of the sections of the Great Wall that tourists visit today are around Beijing, and have been substantially renovated and rebuilt since the Ming era. As impressive as they are, these sections of the wall have little or no connection to the Great Wall of the Qin Dynasty, and they bear little resemblance to the rest of the Great Wall outside Beijing. Very little of the Qin Dynasty wall is even discernable today, and outside Beijing much of the Ming wall has been eroded, demolished, or covered with sandstorms. The imposing square lookout towers, which are such a distinctive image of the wall, are rarely if ever found outside the Beijing area.

Furthermore, not only is the Great Wall not quite as ancient as we might imagine, it is also not quite as much of a wall. The term 'Great Wall' creates an image of a continuous, unbroken barrier, but in fact this has never been the case; the Great Wall has always been a series of unconnected fortifications, with huge gaps in between sections of wall, and others running parallel to one another for miles. Furthermore, many of the sections which are considered to be part of the Great Wall are often not made of 'wall' at all, but instead are geographic barriers: mountains, hills, rivers, valleys and trenches. Although the Great Wall is usually considered to be 5,500 miles long, more than 1,600 miles of this is actually made up of trenches and natural geographic barriers.

And finally, what about the story that the Great Wall of China is the only man-made structure that can be seen from space? This too is a myth. The story seems to have started in a children's book in 1938, more than 30 years before any man had ever set foot on the moon. Astronauts have since confirmed that the Great Wall cannot be seen from the moon, or even from 'low earth orbit', which means an altitude of as just 100 miles up. In fact, according to calculations based on the power of the human eye, it seems that for it to be visible from the moon, the Great Wall would have to be about 70 miles wide, whereas in reality it is no more than 10 metres wide at any point.

Who was Prester John?

In 1165 a very exciting document arrived in Constantinople. It was a letter to the Byzantine Emperor Manuel I, written by Prester John, the leader of a great Christian nation in the

East. 'Prester' was a corruption of the words 'priest' or 'presbyter', and this spiritual leader was believed to be a direct descendant of the Magi, the Three Wise Men who had visited Jesus. Prester John apparently ruled the enormous, peaceful kingdom of the 'three Indias', where there was no crime or vice, and 'honey flows in our land, and milk everywhere abounds'. Prester John's kingdom was a magical place, where rivers ran with gold, and a fountain of youth existed. It was said to have bordered the Garden of Eden itself, and its treasures included a mirror in which every one of the provinces could be observed.

As you'll have no doubt guessed by now, Prester John was a myth. However the story was widely believed, and the letter continued to circulate for centuries, becoming more and more fanciful over the years, as well as changing to reflect the concerns and knowledge of each new age. Prester John's mysterious kingdom was initially located in India, but with the rise of Genghis Khan, the story began to locate him in China and or the Mongol Empire. Later, as explorers failed to find any trace of Prester John's kingdom in Asia, the story shifted to Ethiopia, no doubt because of a lack of knowledge about the geography of Arabia and the Indian Ocean, as Ethiopia was at the time thought to be part of the Asian land mass.

The story of Prester John had significant consequences, as it encouraged numerous missionaries, travellers, and explorers such as Marco Polo, and Giovanni da Montecorvino to venture east, confident that they would soon find themselves under the protection of Prester John and their Christian brothers. The story may thus have hastened contact between the Mongols and the West. More importantly perhaps, the belief in Prester John seems to have been a significant factor in the prolonging of the Crusades. The prospect of a powerful Christian force ready to fight the Muslim hordes from the East was an exciting one. By the early 13th century, Christendom had been almost bankrupted by four great Crusades, but nonetheless a Fifth was launched, in the belief that Prester John would soon come to the rescue. Amazingly, the kingdom of Prester John continued to appear in cartographers' maps as late as the 17th century.

How did the English Navy defeat the invincible Spanish Armada?

For centuries, the British have proudly sung 'Rule, Britannia! Britannia rule the waves!', as Britain's naval dominance is a key part of our national self-image. One of the cornerstones of this belief is England's defeat of the Spanish Armada in 1588, which was the largest sailing force that had ever been seen, being composed of 151 ships, 8,000 sailors and 18,000 soldiers. The defeat of the Armada is seen as a decisive moment in history, as this was the turning point which marked a shift from Spanish dominance of the seas to English dominance, leading to the extraordinary growth of the British Empire in the 17th century.

However, England's naval strength seems to have actually played only a small role in the defeat of the Armada, as none of the main reasons for Spain's defeat can be attributed to England at all. Firstly, the Spanish plan was poorly thought out. The Armada's intention was to sail to the Spanish Netherlands, to collect the Duke of Parma's 30,000-strong army, and then land this army in England as an invasion force. However, Spain had no suitable deepwater ports in northern Europe where the Armada could safely assemble to collect this army, and poor communications meant that it would take many days for the army to assemble, and then be ferried onto the galleons. The plan was therefore unfeasible.

The Armada also suffered from weak leadership. King Philip II of Spain had appointed the highly experienced Àlvaro de Bazàn as commander, but he died in February 1588, and so the job was given instead to the Duke of Medina Sidonia, a wealthy courtier who had no naval experience, but was expected to outwit Britain's experienced commanders Sir Francis Drake, Sir John Hawkins, and Lord Howard. This lack of experience and naval expertise may have led to a number of crucial strategic errors.

On 19 July, the Spanish fleet reached the waters off Cornwall, and a council of war proposed to attack the English fleet, which was trapped in Plymouth Harbour, but Medina Sidonia decided against it. The English then attempted to harry the Spanish along the south coast, but scattered in disarray, and had to spend a day regrouping. Meanwhile the Armada sailed east, and seemed set to assemble in the sheltered waters of the Solent. However, when the reformed English Navy attacked, Medina Sidonia lost his nerve, and sent his fleet back out into the open sea, forcing them to make for Calais.

On July 27, the Armada dropped anchor off Calais, in a defensive crescent formation. The hope was that Parma's army would be ready to meet them there, but in fact the army had not yet even been assembled, and it would take days to have them ready and at the port. At midnight, the English sent eight fireships towards the Armada – fireships were regular warships which had been filled with pitch, tar, brimstone, and gunpowder, and were thus a formidable weapon. In perhaps another indication of weak leadership, the Spanish response to this was to panic and cut their anchors, and the Armada scattered. This now gave the advantage to the English, whose smaller, faster warships could surround and outmanoeuvre the Spanish. At the ensuing Battle of Gravelines, five Spanish ships were lost, but the Armada still posed a major threat, especially as by now the English had run out of ammunition.

At this point, the other significant factor became decisive: the weather. The wind was now coming from the south, which meant that there was little hope for the Armada of returning to Calais to pick up Parma's army. The Spanish decided to return home and regroup, by sailing north to go up and over Scotland, and down the west coast of Ireland. However this was a hazardous and poorly charted route. The Spanish aimed to stay far west of Scotland and Ireland, in the relative safety of the open sea, but at the time there was no way to measure longitude, and so the fleet were driven much further east than they realised. There were also extremely powerful North Atlantic storms in the late 16th century. As a result, many of the Spanish ships were driven onto the lee shore and wrecked. Before this point, the Armada had suffered relatively few casualties, but thanks to the gales 60 ships were destroyed and 5,000 men died, either from drowning, hypothermia, starvation, or violence once they reached the Irish shore. Many more died from disease on the 67 ships that did make it back to Spain.

Although England won a glorious victory, it's hard to point to any decisive moments of English brilliance or strength. The English fleet might well have been trapped in Plymouth Harbour if the Spanish had attacked, and they later scattered in disarray along the south coast. The English Navy may have been victorious at Gravelines, but the Spanish only lost five ships, and if the Armada had decided to sail south to meet the English in battle, the Armada would surely have been victorious, as the English Navy was completely out of ammunition.

Even Queen Elizabeth's inspiring speech at Tilbury, which has become legendary, had no actual impact. On 19

August, Elizabeth famously proclaimed, 'I know I have the body of a weak and feeble woman; but I have the heart and stomach of a King – and a King of England too', but by this point the victory had already effectively been won. The Battle of Gravelines had taken place on 7 August, 12 days beforehand, and by the time of the speech, the Armada had already made it as far north as the Scottish islands of Orkney and Fair Isle, and were suffering badly from thirst and exhaustion. The English Navy had given up its pursuit of the Armada a week beforehand, on the 12 August. Therefore, as inspiring as it surely must have been, Elizabeth's speech actually made no difference at all to the outcome of the conflict.

When was the last successful invasion of England?

It is a well known fact that, despite various attempts, England hasn't been successfully invaded since the Norman Conquest of 1066, led by William the Conqueror. However, the truth is that there was a much more recent conquest, when the Dutch leader William of Orange invaded in 1688, ousting James II, to become King William III. So why do we not talk about the Dutch Conquest of England? The reason is that it is generally considered to have been a revolution rather than an invasion, because William was invited to invade by Parliament, and although he arrived with a considerable army and navy, there was hardly any actual fighting, as most people were keen for William to take over. As a result, the invasion is usually described as The Glorious Revolution or The Bloodless Revolution.

So why were the English so keen for some strange Dutchman to invade their country? The main reason was that he was a Protestant. The English Parliament had been willing to tolerate King James II, despite his Catholic wife Mary of

Modena, because after his death the crown would pass to one of his Protestant daughters, Mary and Anne. However, in 1688 Mary of Modena at last succeeded in giving birth to a son. This raised the prospect of an ongoing Catholic dynasty, which was unacceptable to Parliament and the people, as history had shown that this was certain to lead to instability and turmoil, and most likely bloodshed and persecutions.

In response, England's two leading political parties, the Tories and the Whigs, united to resolve the crisis, by having the crown pass to James's Protestant daughter, Mary, who was the wife of Dutch prince William of Orange. Parliament thus invited William to invade, promising him their support. In October 1688, William arrived with his army of 40,000, aboard a fleet around 2-3 times the size of the Spanish Armada. After landing without incident at Torbay in Devon, the army marched slowly to London, encountering almost no resistance. Unable to muster an army, James fled, to Catholic France.

Now that James seemed to be out of the way, there were still some legal and constitutional issues to address. James was still arguably the rightful and incumbent king, which meant that technically no parliament could be called. In the end, a decision was made that James had effectively abdicated his throne by leaving the country. Parliament now had to decide who would be the new monarch. William was only fourth in the line of succession, behind James's newborn son, William's own wife Mary, and Mary's sister Anne. Parliament considered making Mary queen, or giving William the title of Regent, ruling in the place of James II, but William was insistent that he would only stay in England if he was made king. As a result, a face-saving solution was found. William and Mary would rule jointly, giving the impression that the Stuart line of descent was intact, even though in practice William would rule as king.

Alongside James's religion, Parliament's other main problem with him had been his belief in the Divine Right of Kings, which held that kings were appointed by God, and therefore not answerable to Parliament, the people, or anyone else. James's rule had been characterised by efforts to undermine, dismiss, and weaken Parliament. In one of the most significant moments in English history, William was required to accept a Bill of Rights, if he was to be handed the crown. By accepting the Bill of Rights, William was agreeing to severe restrictions of royal power. From now on, the monarch would not be able to raise taxes, raise an army, or ignore or suspend Parliament's laws. Parliaments would be determined by free and frequent elections, and the monarch could not be a Catholic, or marry a Catholic. This marked the beginning of England's constitutional monarchy, a system which has lasted successfully ever since.

When was the first world war?

Of course, most people know that World War One was fought between 1914-1918, but that conflict was not in fact the first 'world war' to take place. According to Winston Churchill, the first world war was actually the Seven Years' War of 1756-1763, which was a conflict fought primarily between the empires of Britain and France, but which also involved a great many of the world's other powers, and was fought over an unprecedented, global canvass.

The hostilities actually began in 1754, as Britain and France fought for control of the Ohio valley, which was key to their respective colonial expansion plans in North America. In this, Britain was supported by her colonial militias, whose leaders included a young lieutenant colonel by the name of George Washington. This conflict is known in the US as the French and Indian War, and in Canada as the War of Conquest.

The other important precursor to the war was the Wars of Austrian Succession, which had been fought from 1740-1748, and in which King Frederick II of Prussia had captured the wealthy province of Schleswig from Austria. Frederick was perhaps the greatest military leader of the age, and was consequently known as Frederick the Great. One outcome of this war was that Austria was significantly weakened.

In early 1756, the nations began to shift their longheld alliances, in anticipation of possible war, in what became known as the Diplomatic Revolution. Previously, Britain had allied with Austria, against the united front of France and Prussia. However, Britain no longer saw the weakened Austria as a useful ally, as it was unable to pose a meaningful threat to France. King George II therefore considered that Prussia would be a more suitable ally, in that it would be able to effectively defend George's home state of Hanover. France meanwhile allied with Austria, along with Russia and Sweden, all of which felt threatened by the growing power of Frederick's Prussia. Later in the war, Portugal joined the British side, with Spain joining the French. On 18 May 1756 war was formally declared between England and France, and soon afterwards France besieged and then successfully invaded Minorca, a small island off the Spanish coast. Over the next seven years, fighting would take place in North America, Europe, the Caribbean, India, Africa, and the Philippines.

Britain had the most powerful navy in the world, and as a result won major gains in North America (including Canada) and India, as well as gaining Senegal, Guadeloupe, and the important cities of Havana and Manila, leaving Britain as the world's dominant colonial power. Prussia, despite being the smallest of the continental powers, nonetheless managed to defend all of its previous gains, even though it had to fight on as many as four fronts simultaneously, being attacked from the west by France, the east by Russia, the south by Austria, and the north by Sweden. As a result, Prussia emerged from the war as arguably the strongest of the continental powers, despite having seemed at times close to defeat. This was thanks to the inspired leadership of Frederick the Great, considerable financial and military support from Britain, and at one point Russia temporarily switching sides, when the Empress Elizabeth died, to be replaced by the Prussophile Peter III.

So if the Seven Years' War was actually the first world war, why was the conflict of 1914-1918 given that name? Confusingly, the explanation is that the 1914-1918 war wasn't called the first world war either, at least not at the time. While it was taking place, it was generally known as The Great War, as well as other names including The Kaiser's War, and The War To End All Wars. It was only in the late 1930s, when war with Nazi Germany became imminent, that people began to describe this new war as 'World War Two', making the Great War retrospectively by definition 'World War One'. Although the Seven Years' War had taken place on a global scale, it had only resulted in around 900,000 to 1.4 million deaths, compared with the 9 million killed in the Great War (and the 50-70 million who would die in World War Two). As such, the Seven Years' War was not felt to be of the same magnitude as the two wars now dubbed 'world wars', even though it was technically the first global war.

How big was the proposed tax increase that led to the Boston Tea Party?

It is well known that the Boston Tea Party was a protest against tea duties, which were being imposed on the American colonies by the British government. In response, in 1773 a group of around 40-50 early American patriots dressed up as Mohawk Indians, stormed onto the three tea ships which were waiting in Boston Harbor, and dumped 343 chests of tea into the sea in protest. Britain sensed that it was losing control at this point, and so imposed the Coercive Acts, closing Boston Harbor, and revoking the Massachusetts charter. In response, the colonies united, by forming the First Continental Congress and boycotting British goods, in a process which soon escalated into the American War of Independence.

The Boston Tea Party is now seen as a defining moment in American history, and a powerful symbol of political protest. The name 'Tea Party' has of course recently gained a new lease of life, as the name of the rapidly-growing right-wing movement whose most prominent figure is presidential candidate Sarah Palin. The movement's chief goals are to shrink the size of government and to reduce taxes, and the movement thus sees itself as being to some extent a successor to the Boston Tea Party, which was also a protest about tax.

The irony is that the Boston Tea Party was not in fact incited by a tax increase at all, but by a tax cut. The protest was a response to Britain's 1773 Tea Act, which effectively cut the tax on tea coming into the colonies by a massive 75 percent, from 12 pence per pound to just 3 pence per pound. The main goal of the act was to help the struggling East India Company offload 18 million pounds of surplus tea, and so the result of this tax cut would be that tea would become even cheaper in the colonies than it was in Britain, from where it was being imported.

So why were the patriots so outraged by a tax cut? The answer is that the Boston Tea Party was not about the level of taxes at all, but about the principle of them. Britain had consistently failed to levy any meaningful level of taxation from the colonies, and in 1770 had been forced to remove import taxes on all goods except tea, after protests against the 1767 Townshend Revenue Act. All that was left was the tax on tea, which would raise only a negligible sum, but the British government was determined to keep the tax, to maintain the precedent that Britain had the theoretical right to tax America, even if so far it had in practice been unable to do so.

There was also another reason why Britain was keen to maintain tea duties, which was that the revenue raised was used to pay colonial officials. The amount of money in question was very small, but again it was a matter of principle: Britain wanted the colonial officials to be paid by Parliament, which meant that they would be dependant on the British government, and hopefully therefore loyal.

American patriots were outraged by the Tea Act because it had been imposed on them without consultation, and so the issue was one of self-governance. The patriots argued that there should be 'no more taxation without representation' – this was the law in Britain, and so as British subjects, they argued, the same should apply in the colonies. The protestors were also concerned about the issue of colonial officials being dependent upon Parliament, as this was felt to undermine colonial rights.

Tea was also an ideal focus for protest, as it was powerfully symbolic, and generated strong opinions. Tea, with its fancy rituals and dainty crockery, was seen to represent the snooty arrogance of the British Parliament, and an out-dated kind of social hierarchy which did not apply in the New World. Many Puritans also argued that tea was a dangerous stimulant, which was causing a pernicious decline in Western physical and mental well-being. Hostility to tea also played to protectionist, anti-foreign sentiments.

Interestingly, although the Boston Tea Party is seen today as a jubilant event to be celebrated and commemorated, this wasn't the case at the time. For 50 years afterwards, the event was largely ignored, as it was essentially an act of lawless vandalism, imbued with revolutionary fervour, involving the destruction of property, none of which were seen as suit-able qualities to be celebrated in the early years of the United States. It was only years later, as time had the effect of taking the sting out of the story, that the Boston Tea Party began to be woven into the nation's cultural identity.

What caused the Mutiny On The Bounty?

In 1789 naval Lieutenant William Bligh led the Bounty on an expedition to Tahiti, to collect stores of breadfruit plants, and then transport them to the West Indies, where they would provide a new, cheap, nutritious foodstuff to feed the colony's slaves. However, having spent five months in Tahiti waiting for the plants to ripen sufficiently for transportation, the crew of the Bounty mutinied. Bligh and 18 loyal supporters were set adrift on a 23 foot launch, with only enough rations for five days. In an amazing feat of seamanship, Bligh managed to navigate his way to Timor over a period of 48 days, a journey of 3,618 miles, without charts or a compass. He then returned to Britain, where he notified the Admiralty of the mutiny, and was himself cleared of any wrongdoing.

But why did the mutiny take place? The standard account is well known, as it has been documented in numerous books and films. In this version, Captain Bligh is a hidebound tyrant, whose strictness and cruelty become unbearable, as he withholds rations, and liberally dispenses floggings, until the noble mutineers, led by the young, handsome Fletcher Christian, are forced to take action. In this Hollywood account, Bligh is played by uptight, middle-aged, headmasterly types such as Anthony Hopkins and Trevor Howard, while Christian is played by rugged young heartthrobs such as Marlon Brando, Mel Gibson, and Errol Flynn.

In fact, the evidence suggests that, by the standards of the time, Bligh was an unusually liberal and easy-going captain, and this may have been the real problem, as his authority seems to have slipped as a result. Floggings were the standard method of punishment at sea, but the Bounty's voyage was notable for Bligh flogging proportionately fewer of his crew than any other Pacific captain of the eighteenth century. Bligh scolded when other captains would have flogged, and flogged when other captains would have hanged.

It turns out that almost every detail of the Hollywood caricature is wrong. Bligh was not a middle-aged, upper class martinet oppressing Fletcher Christian, the earthy man of the people. On the contrary, Bligh was only 33, and from a modest background, while Christian's family were gentry, and could trace their roots back to Edward I and William the Conqueror. Bligh took a modern, liberal approach to his crew, taking great care over their diet, sanitation, and exercise, and as a result there was not a single case of scurvy on board. Bligh strove to break down the barriers between ranks, often inviting senior crew to dine with him in his private quarters. There was no purser on board, so Bligh would take on this role himself, lending and advancing money to many of the crew, including Christian on several occasions.

The natural conclusion to be drawn is that, rather than being too strict with his crew, Bligh was in fact too lenient. The lack of punishment and strict hierarchy may well have undermined the crew's confidence and respect for Bligh's authority. After spending five months in the paradise of Tahiti, where many of the crew took wives, and enjoyed a life of unprecedented pleasure, comfort, and sexual freedom, it is perhaps not surprising that they lacked enthusiasm for another long, arduous, and dangerous voyage, especially now that their rations and living quarters would now be even more restricted, because of the cargo of breadfruit plants.

It seems that Bligh was placed in an impossible position. Although we know him as Captain Bligh, one of the most important facts is that he wasn't a captain. Bligh was only a lieutenant in the navy, and was refused the rank of captain for the Bounty expedition, despite being put in charge. He was given no Royal Marines for the voyage, who would normally be responsible for keeping order among the crew, and he lacked the physical stature and reputation of his mentor, Captain James Cook. As a result of these handicaps, maintaining discipline was always likely to be a challenge, even without the temptations of Tahiti. William Bligh should therefore be remembered not as the petty tyrant of Hollywood films, but as a brilliant seaman and navigator, whose career included many other great triumphs after his return from Tahiti, including a repeat of the Bounty expedition, which this time succeeded in taking breadfruit plants to the West Indies, where they continue to thrive as a popular foodstuff to this day.

3

SAUCY SAGAS

'Real solemn history, I cannot be interested in. The quarrels of popes and kings, with wars or pestilences, in every page; the men all so good for nothing, and hardly any women at all, it is very tiresome.'

Northanger Abbey, Jane Austen (1775-1817)

How did King Eadwig celebrate his coronation?

Eadwig became the King of England in the year 955 AD, after the death of his uncle King Eadred, who had defeated the Viking Eric Bloodaxe, and driven the Danes out of England. He was known as 'Eadwig the Fair' on account of his exceptional good looks, and was just fifteen years old when he came to the throne, so it is perhaps unsurprising that he shared the main preoccupation of most fifteen year old boys, namely sex. After the coronation, Eadwig slipped away from the celebratory banquet. When the stern Abbot of Glastonbury, St Dunstan, went looking for him, he found him in bed with two women: a young noblewoman named Aelfgifu, and her mother, Aethelgifu.

St Dunstan was infuriated by this sordid scene, and physically dragged the King back to the solemn feast, and forced him to denounce Aelfgifu as a 'strumpet'. This manhandling of the King was a bad move, and St Dunstan soon realised that he had overstepped the mark, and went into hiding in the sanctuary of his monastery. However Eadwig, who was by now being egged on by the furious Aethelgifu, showed little concern for religious protocol, as he and his men pursued St Dunstan, and sacked the monastery. St Dunstan managed to escape and flee the country, and would remain in exile until Eadwig's death.

Eadwig's feud with Dunstan meant that his reign was marked by constant conflict with the church and nobility. Eadwig married Aelfgifu soon after his coronation, but their marriage was annulled against their will by Archbishop Odo, on the dubious grounds that the pair were too closely related. It's true that Eadwig and Aelfgifu were distant cousins, but no more than many other couples in England, which at the time had a population of around one million. In terms of degrees of consanguinity, Queen Elizabeth II and Prince Philip are more closely related than Eadwig and Aelfgifu were. Aelfgifu went on to become a major landowner and church benefactor, who was described as being 'the most illustrious of women'.

Eadwig's reign descended into civil war, as he was challenged by his brother Edgar, who had the support of Dunstan and the church. Eadwig died in 959, at the age of just 19, in unknown circumstances. He was succeeded by Edgar, whose reign was far more stable, and who was consequently known as Edgar the Peaceable. However, Edgar seems to have been just as randy as his older brother, taking numerous mistresses, and even having an illegitimate child with a nun whom he was said to have abducted. Edgar's lascivious behaviour so outraged St Dunstan that he refused to crown him until he mended his ways. In the end, Edgar wasn't crowned until the year 973, towards the end of his reign, fourteen years after he had come to power, which suggests that Dunstan's pleas had made little impact.

Why did Lady Godiva ride naked through the streets of Coventry?

Lady Godiva was the wife of Leofric, Earl of Mercia, who was one of the most powerful men in England in the 11th century. She also seems to have been wealthy and power-ful in her own right, as she was one of the leading reli-gious benefactors of the period, founding and supporting a number of monasteries. After the Norman conquest, Lady Godiva was one of the few Anglo-Saxons to be mentioned in the Domesday Book, and the only woman to remain a major landholder. Leofric died before the Norman Con-quest, in 1057.

Today of course Lady Godiva is chiefly remembered for her famously shocking naked horseback ride through the centre of Coventry. But why did she do it? According to the legend, it was to get her husband to lower his oppressive regime of taxes, which were suffocating the poor townspeo-ple. Having resisted numerous pleas from his kind-hearted wife, the Earl eventually retorted that he would remove the taxes the day she rode naked through the town. Lady Godiva called his bluff, and the Earl was as good as his word, removing all taxes from the people, leaving only those levied on horses. Lady Godiva thus became a folk hero, seen as a defender of the people, and she is still celebrated to this day in Coventry, where her statue stands in the centre of town, and her image is used as the logo for the City Council.

But is there actually any truth to this story? Sadly, it seems unlikely. There was a real Lady Godiva, and she was a generous religious benefactor and a wealthy landowner, but there is no surviving reference to her famous procession from within her lifetime. The story seems to have first appeared in the Latin chronicle *Flores Historiarum* (which means Flowers of History), in manuscripts written by Roger of Wendover in the early 13th century, around 150 years after Lady Godiva's death. Roger of Wendover is today regarded more as a collector of folklore than a reliable historian, which adds to the impression that the story is apocryphal.

Over the centuries, other details have been added to the story. A version produced in the 17th century described Lady Godiva as having extremely long, golden hair, with which she covered her naked body, so that no one could actually see any rude bits. Another version states that before taking the procession she ordered the townspeople to stay indoors and shut their windows, so that no one would see her naked. According to this version of the story, all the townspeople complied, except for one voyeur, a tailor called Tom, who bored a hole in his shutters so that he could see the exciting spectacle, but as a punishment he was struck blind by the gods. This story gave rise to the term 'Peeping Tom'.

Why was Eleanor of Aquitaine in such a rush to get married?

Eleanor of Aquitaine was one of the most influential women of the High Middle Ages. She married twice, first to Louis VII of France, and then to Henry of Anjou, who went on to become Henry II of England, and so Eleanor was at different times queen of both France and England. She was also effectively the sole ruler of England for almost all of the reign of her son Richard the Lionheart, as she acted as regent while he spent most of his reign crusading overseas. Eleanor's marriages were conducted at great haste, as a consequence of her great wealth. When her father and her brother died in 1137, the 15-year old Eleanor became the Duchess of Aquitaine, the largest province of France, which comprised around a third of the entire country. This meant she immediately became the wealthiest and most eligible heiress in Europe.

So why, you may wonder, did her wealth mean that she had to get married quickly? Surely, being independently rich and powerful ought to have been liberating, giving Eleanor the freedom to make her own choices? Well, the reason Eleanor had to marry quickly is that this was an era when it was quite common for wealthy, unmarried women to be kidnapped and forced into marriage, resulting in the effective loss of all their wealth and power. As the richest woman in Europe, Eleanor was the perfect target for a kidnapping, and so it was imperative that she should be safely married to someone suitable as quickly as possible.

Her father's will had stipulated that, on his death, Eleanor should be taken under the protection of King Louis VI of France, who would act as her guardian. Louis quickly married Eleanor off to his son, who was also called Louis, but this marriage was fraught with conflict, and exacerbated by their failure to conceive a son. In 1152 the marriage was annulled, on the grounds that they were too closely related, being third cousins once removed. By this point, Eleanor was already involved in an affair with Henry of Anjou, and she now summoned him to marry her as quickly as possible, despite the fact that Henry was actually an even closer blood relation than Louis had been. In the six weeks between the annulment and her marriage to Henry, Eleanor had to escape at least two kidnapping attempts from French lords, as she made her way back to Poitiers.

However, Eleanor was far more than simply a wealthy possession in this medieval soap opera, as she was a fascinating and feisty character in her own right. She faced considerable disapproval at the French court after her marriage to Louis, as the beautiful new Queen was seen to be far too flighty, spirited, and immodest for courtly tastes. When Louis set out on the Second Crusade, Eleanor insisted on going with him, with 300 of her ladies in attendance, all clad in armour and carrying lances. During the Crusade, she took a key role in determining strategy, and fell out with her husband as a result. Louis was an incompetent tactician, and so instead Eleanor favoured the plans of her uncle, Raymond of Poitiers, with whom she was said to be having a scandalous affair, an affair which was both adulterous and incestuous. As Eleanor continued to defy her husband, Louis had her imprisoned, which effectively marked the end of their marriage.

Eleanor is also remembered for another scandalous story concerning the Crusades, although it seems likely that this one is probably apocryphal. According to some accounts, Eleanor and her ladies in waiting marched into the Holy Land dressed as Amazons, with Eleanor riding bare-breasted, to dazzle and intimidate the enemy. Sadly, there are no surviving contemporary sources to confirm this story, but it doesn't sound completely out of character for this extraordinary and fearless woman.

How was the wedding night of Humphrey of Toron interrupted?

In 1183, the young nobleman Humphrey IV of Toron married Princess Isabella of Jerusalem. Humphrey was around

16-17 years old, while Isabella was just 11. The wedding took place at the Castle of Kerak, in the Kingdom of Jerusalem, which was one of the largest and most impregnable fortresses of the crusading era. Kerak was ruled by Raynald of Châtillon, Humphrey's stepfather, who was one of the most ruthless and controversial figures of the age. Raynald was a great warrior, who was notionally a Christian, although this didn't stop him from attacking Christian neighbours when it suited him. He was a maverick who pursued his own goals, with a history of making audacious attacks on the Muslim Empire of Saladin, and ignoring truces that had been agreed between the Christian and Muslim worlds.

In 1183, Raynald once again decided to ignore an existing truce, and captured the town of Aqaba, in present-day Jordan, which gave him a powerful base from which to attack Mecca, the holiest city in all of Islam. In retaliation, Saladin laid siege to the Castle of Kerak, using siege towers to mount the walls, and catapults to rain missiles on the inhabitants within. However, this was the night of Humphrey and Isabella's wedding, and so Humphrey's mother, Stephanie of Milly, sent out a message to Saladin, along with some food from the wedding banquet. The message explained that this was the young couple's wedding night, and asked Saladin to remember the affection they had shared when he had been a prisoner in the castle, and had carried the young Stephanie in his arms. In response, Saladin sent a reply, asking which tower the couple were staying in. When he got the answer, he ordered his troops to stop their bombardment of this particular tower, so that the couple could enjoy their wedding night in peace. Meanwhile, inside the castle the wedding party continued, while great rocks smashed against the walls, and the battle raged outside.

This spirit of chivalry was not to last. The siege was raised when Isabella's father arrived with a relief force, and another truce was agreed. This was soon broken when, in 1186, Raynald attacked an Islamic caravan travelling from Cairo to Damascus, possibly in an attempt to kidnap Saladin's sister. Saladin vowed that he would kill Raynald himself if he ever took him prisoner. A year later, Saladin defeated the bulk of the crusading forces at the Battle of Hattin, taking back Jerusalem, which had been held by the Christians for 88 years, and Raynald was taken as one of a number of prominent prisoners. Saladin summoned his defeated rival, and told him off for repeatedly breaking his pledges. Raynald replied, 'Kings have always acted thus. I did nothing more.' Saladin later executed Raynald personally, cutting off his head with his sword. Seeing this, King Guy of Jerusalem was terrified that he would be next, but Saladin reassured him, 'A king does not kill a king; but that man had transgressed all bounds, and therefore did I treat him thus.'

For what crime was Joan of Arc burned at the stake?

The story of Joan of Arc is one of the most extraordinary in all of history. Joan was born into a lowly farming family, and yet by the age of just 17 she had somehow become the leader of the French army, winning a number of astonishing victories against the previously dominant English forces. After being captured, she was put on trial by the English at Rouen, and burned alive at the stake, at the age of just 19.

It was at the age of 13 that Joan's life started to change. Until this point, she had been a fairly conventional farm girl, if unusually pious. Then one day she had a strange vision, in which the Archangel Michael appeared, and told her she would have to raise an army to drive the English out of France. At this point, France had been ravaged by the Hundred Years' War for more than three generations, and England held much of northern France, including Burgundy, where Joan lived. Joan continued to hear voices, who identified themselves as Saint Catherine, Saint Margaret, and the Archangel Michael, who instructed her that she must dress up as a man, persuade the Dauphin to give her an army, and then lead them into battle herself. She described the voices as coming from the direction of the church, always accompanied by a strange light.

In 1429, at the age of 16, she travelled to the nearby town of Vaucouleurs, to try and win support from the local officials. After telling them about a vision which successfully predicted the French defeat at the Battle of Herrings, she was given an armed guard, and taken to the Dauphin himself. She now had to prove herself all over again, which she did by convincing a series of doctors and clerics of her authenticity and sincerity, by recognising the first Dauphin presented to her as an impostor, and then by whispering the Dauphin's guilty secret in his ear. There were some doubts about the Dauphin's legitimacy, as his mother was believed to have had an affair with the Duke of Orléans, and so it's possible Joan may have whispered something in relation to this, and thus won the Dauphin's confidence. Joan then predicted that she would lift the siege of Orléans, retake Rheims, and then crown the Dauphin there as King Charles VII.

Amazingly, the Dauphin agreed to raise an army for Joan, which she then commanded and led to the besieged city of Orléans. At this point, France had suffered a long series of humiliating defeats, which helps to explain why Charles would even consider such a bizarre and desperate move. Joan's army entered Orléans on 30 April 1429, and within just 9 days the surrounding forts had been retaken, and the siege lifted, as the troops moved at a breathtaking pace, inspired by the religious fervour of their strange young commander. Joan's army pressed on, winning a series of stunning victories, so that by July, they had reached the pivotal, symbolic city of Rheims, which was traditionally where French kings were crowned. Just as Joan had foretold, the Dauphin was now crowned King Charles VII of France at Rheims.

However, in September 1429, the tide of French victories began to turn. Joan's army were defeated in an attempt to take Paris, and she suffered an arrow through the thigh and had to be carried from the battlefield. The following spring, Joan's visions were telling her that she would soon be captured, and again she was proven correct, when her army became trapped by the Burgundian forces, and she was taken as a prisoner. At this point, many felt Charles should have done more to recover her, but he appears to have made no attempt to rescue or ransom her, and so she was sold to the English. In their custody, she was taken to Rouen, to be tried by an ecclesiastical court.

The trial was a sham, in which Joan was not allowed to make a case to defend herself, and was molested and abused by her English guards. Even so, the brilliance of her testimony was such that she began to win over the spectators and witnesses. At one point she was asked if she knew she was in God's grace. This was a trick question, as an answer of 'yes' would have been seen as heresy, whereas saying 'no' would have sounded like an admission of guilt. However, Joan's witty and elegant response foiled her interrogators, as she replied, 'If I am not, may God put me there; and if I am, may God so keep me.'

Joan's compelling performance was becoming an embarrassment to the English, and so the trial was moved into the prison, out of public view. After a year of mistreatment and subterfuge, Joan was sentenced to life imprisonment, having finally submitted to sign a retraction. However, this was not enough for the English, who insisted that she had to be executed, perhaps fearful of the potential effect on the French troops if she was ever to reappear. A pretext was soon found, when Joan was caught wearing men's clothes, which was taken to mean that she had relapsed into heresy. The next day, she was burned at the stake, and then her remains were repeatedly burned, to ensure that there were no relics left for followers to venerate.

It's not clear why Joan was wearing men's clothes, but based on later testimony it seems to have been either a strategy to protect herself from rape, or simply a trap which had been laid for her, when all her other clothes were stolen by the guards. And so, for the crime of cross-dressing, Joan of Arc was convicted of heresy and burned alive.

How did Nell Gwyn get the better of a rival courtesan?

Nell Gwyn was one of the many mistresses of England's King Charles II, and the only one who was well loved by the public. On one famous occasion, her carriage was attacked by a group of angry protestors, who thought it contained Gwyn's rival, Charles's Catholic mistress Louise de Kérouaille. Gwyn leaned her head out of the coach window, and smilingly explained, 'Good people, you are mistaken. I am the *Protestant* whore.'

Charles had developed a taste for illicit sex during his time in exile in Europe, after his father Charles I had been executed during the English Civil War, and replaced by a republican Commonwealth led by Oliver Cromwell. After the restoration of the monarchy in 1660, the newly crowned King Charles II was keen to continue his life of debauchery and pleasure, and the dalliances of the 'Merrie Monarch' were seen to capture the nation's joyful, liberated mood, after the repressive Puritanism of the Cromwell reign.

Despite being married, Charles was openly involved with a series of mistresses, and had a particular fondness for actresses. After the restoration, Charles had reopened the theatres, and for the first time women were allowed to perform on stage, in another sign of the new, carefree spirit of the age. Charles was a keen theatregoer, who particularly enjoyed the opportunity to meet attractive young actresses. One of his long-term mistresses was the actress Moll Davis, whom he met in around 1667, at a time when actresses seem to have often also been prostitutes or courtesans. Moll Davis was not well loved by the public, as she was seen to be greedy and vulgar, flaunting the wealth she gained from her association with the King. The wife of diarist Samuel Pepys described her as, 'The most impertinent slut in the world.'

Moll Davis soon found she had a rival in Nell Gwyn, who was a celebrated actress, as well as being a courtesan. Gwyn had risen from humble beginnings in London's East End to find fame through her comic performances in the new genre of 'restoration comedy', aided by a series of advantageous liaisons. After attracting the attention of the King, who called her 'pretty, witty Nell', she learned that Moll Davis was due to call on him one night, and so decided to make some mischief. She met Davis for tea and cakes, but spiked her rival's cake with the laxative jalap. When the unfortunate Davis found she was unable to make her assignation with the King, Gwyn went in her place. Soon after this, Davis was dismissed by Charles, and Nell became his new favourite.

Despite her profession, Nell Gwyn became well-loved by the English public, as she was seen to be loyal, spirited, and witty. Other courtesans were generally unfaithful, but Gwyn was completely loyal to Charles, and even punched the Duke of Buckingham on the ear when he dared to try and kiss her. She was concerned for the fate of former servicemen, after seeing an old soldier pitifully begging in the street, and so she encouraged Charles to build the Royal Hospital in Chelsea. Unlike her rivals, she wasn't demanding or temperamental, and she didn't flaunt the wealth she gained from her relationship, but instead tried to turn her homes into a sanctuary where Charles could relax and feel at home. It was therefore said that Gwyn was the only one of Charles' mistresses who actually loved him.

Charles failed to produce any legitimate heirs, even though he openly acknowledged at least 12 illegitimate children, and many of these were given dukedoms or earldoms. In a strange twist, two of Charles's illegitimate sons, who became the dukes of Grafton and Richmond respectively, were ancestors of Diana, Princess of Wales. This means that if Prince William ever becomes king, he will be the first English monarch to be descended from Charles II. Another bizarre detail is that Samantha Cameron, the wife of the British Prime Minister David Cameron, is descended from Nell Gwyn, who is her great-great-great-great-great-great-great-great grandmother.

Why were prizefighters stationed outside Westminster Abbey on the occasion of King George IV's coronation?

The answer is that they were there to keep out his wife Caroline, whom he hated, and had banned from attending. George and Caroline had one of the most miserable marriages of any British monarch. George had only agreed to marry Caroline in the first place because he had run up enormous debts, as a result of his extravagant lifestyle, and Parliament would only advance him more money if he agreed to marry, with a view to providing an heir. In fact, George was already married, to a Catholic commoner named Maria Fitzherbert, but the government decided to keep this quiet, and considered the marriage to be invalid, on the dubious grounds that George was required to get his father's permission to marry, and had not done so.

George reluctantly agreed to Parliament's plan, and so in 1795 Caroline of Brunswick was brought over to England, being the most eligible Protestant princess available. Upon meeting his new bride, it's fair to say that George wasn't enamoured, declaring, 'I am not well; pray get me a glass of brandy.' Caroline was said to be a coarse, unattractive, and uneducated woman, who paid insufficient attention to her personal hygiene. Caroline meanwhile was equally disappointed at the match she had made, commenting, '[He is] very fat and he's nothing like as handsome as his portrait.'

After their meeting, George is said to have gone on a three-day brandy binge until the wedding, and then spent the wedding night passed out on the bedroom floor, with his head in the hearth. In the morning, he managed to consummate the marriage, apparently with the aid of more alcohol, 'to conquer my person and overcome the disgust of her person.' In the first two days of the marriage, the pair managed to conceive an heir, Princess Charlotte, but having done so the pair would never sleep together again.

George and Caroline soon began living entirely separate lives, and both became involved in affairs with other people. Caroline adopted a number of young children, and it was alleged that one of them, a three-month-old boy named William Austin, was her illegitimate child. In response to this scandalous allegation, Parliament began what it called the 'Delicate Investigation', but it soon became clear that the claim was unfounded. By 1811, George's father King George III had become fully insane, and so George was appointed as Regent. Caroline was forced into exile in Italy, where she was believed to have begun an affair with a married servant, Bartolomeo Pergami.

On 29 June 1820, George III finally died, and so the Prince Regent began to prepare for his coronation. The only problem was his wife, who was enormously popular with the British public, who viewed her as an innocent, wronged woman, while they despised the obese, extravagant Prince. George tried to get Parliament to force through a divorce, but the MPs were fearful of the public reaction, knowing that any divorce proceedings would reveal just as many of George's embarrassing indiscretions as Caroline's.

After a delay of more than a year, George finally gave up on the idea of divorce, and the coronation of King George IV took place on 19 July 1821. Outside Westminster Abbey, he arranged for prizefighters to stand guard, disguised as pages, to keep out unwanted guests, which chiefly meant Caroline. However, Caroline was about to become the Queen of England, and she had no intention of missing out on her big day. She arrived at the Abbey, and attempted to enter first through the East Cloister, and then the West Cloister, but was turned away each time. She then tried to get in through Westminster Hall, which was packed with guests, but the door was slammed in her face, and the guards held bayonets under her chin, forcing her to retreat.

It was a humiliating, undignified spectacle, and as a result Caroline lost some of her popularity. That night, she fell sick, and over the following three weeks her condition quickly deteriorated. She died on 7 August 1821, having repeatedly stated her belief that she had been poisoned. The public were incensed at her treatment. The Prime Minister Lord Liverpool, fearful of public unrest, arranged for her funeral procession to avoid passing through London, but an angry mob blocked the intended, circuitous route, and fought with soldiers, with two people killed in the angry scenes. Eventually, the police submitted, and the cortège was allowed to pass through the city.

By contrast, when George died in 1830, his obituary in The Times newspaper was felt by many to sum up the national mood. It read, 'There never was an individual less regretted by his fellow-creatures than this deceased king... If he ever had a friend – a devoted friend in any rank of life – we protest that the name of him or her never reached us.'

Why was Queen Victoria such a prude?

Today, Queen Victoria is well known to have been a narrow-minded prude, whose repressive attitude to sexual matters had a dramatic effect on English culture which is still powerfully felt today. The Victorian era, we are told, was one in which table legs had to be covered up, for fear that a shapely leg could stimulate erotic feelings, and women at the beach would trundle to the sea in 'bathing machines', which were a kind of four-wheeled shed, so that they could swim 'with the strictest delicacy', without the shame of being seen publicly in their bathing costume. The phrase most associated with Queen Victoria herself was the stern, upright, 'We are not amused', and she is even believed to have refused to pass a law banning lesbianism, not because she was liberal-minded when it came to homosexuality, but because she didn't believe there was such a thing as a lesbian, stating simply, 'Women do not do such things.'

However, Victoria was not always the straight-laced, sexless figure that she came to embody. As a young woman, she was known to be sensual, girlish, and keenly interested in romance, with a particular weakness for good-looking men. On Albert's first visits, Victoria would watch him arrive from the top of the stairs, confiding to her journal, 'It was with some emotion that I beheld Albert, who is *beautiful*.' After they married, she described her wedding night in gushing terms, 'It was a gratifying and bewildering experience. I never, never spent such an evening. His excessive love and affection gave me feelings of heavenly love and happiness. He clasped me in his arms and we kissed each other again and again.' Another night, she simply wrote, 'We did not sleep much.'

After her marriage, Victoria's sensuality seems to have only increased. Victoria frequently gave Albert paintings of attractive nude women as gifts, and even commissioned a provocative portrait of herself, known as the 'secret picture', in which she is reclining seductively on a red cushion, with her long hair draped across her chest. The couple had nine children, with a gap of no more than two years between each birth, and when her doctor advised her against any more pregnancies, she exclaimed, 'What? No more fun in bed? Oh God!'.

After Albert's death, we tend to think of Victoria withdrawing completely from public life, and devoting herself to mourning, and commissioning memorials to her beloved husband, such as the Royal Albert Hall. The story goes that she draped so much black crepe in the halls and rooms of Windsor Castle that she used up the nation's entire stocks. However, even after Albert's death, Victoria remained romantically active, and quite possibly sexually active too. Her love affair with her personal attendant John Brown is well known – she even secretly arranged for his photograph, his mother's ring, and a lock of his hair to be placed in her coffin on her death – but she also became close to Prime Minister Benjamin Disraeli, and a young Indian servant named Abdul Karim.

It is true that the Victorian Era was one of strict morality, and a repressive attitude towards sex, but this did not reflect Victoria's own nature. For example, it's true that references to lesbianism were removed from the bill banning homosexuality, but it was not because of Victoria's influence; it was because MPs were concerned that publicising the existence of lesbianism might encourage women to take it up. In fact, if any one person can be said to have been responsible for the stern morality of the period, it was more likely to have been Victoria's husband, the stern, rational Prince Albert. Albert's parents had had a turbulent marriage, with both having affairs. This led to their divorce, and as a result Albert's mother disappeared from his life when he was just five years old, and this loss is known to have had a damaging effect on him. After marrying Victoria, Albert would criticise her for her uninhibited behaviour, and encourage her to behave in a more appropriate, buttoned down manner.

Albert and Victoria were also aware that the previous Hanoverian monarchs had been seen as discrediting and cheapening the monarchy through their various sexual and financial scandals. George IV, in particular, had been extremely unpopular, as he was (rightly) seen as a dissolute playboy, who showed little interest in the business of government, and ran up enormous debts. By the time of Victoria's accession to the throne, the monarchy was increasingly becoming a symbolic institution, with limited political influence, and so Victoria and Albert steered the role into that of a moral, ceremonial figurehead, which sought to be seen as above politics entirely.

What was the 'Castle of Love'?

The 'Castle of Love' was a rather theatrical scheme which took place in the tiny coastal city of Fiume in 1920, which was located on the border between Italy and Yugoslavia (although Yugoslavia at the time was known by the rather wordier name of the Kingdom of Serbs, Croats and Slovenes). In 1919, Fiume had been invaded by the soldier-poet Gabriele D'Annunzio, who declared it to be an independent republic. As a leader, D'Annunzio had a great number of qualities, but administration was not one of them, and within weeks of the invasion, Fiume had descended into almost complete anarchy. D'Annunzio, the self-style 'Duce', seemed to have little interest in dealing with the mundane issues of government, as he was far too pre-occupied with his mistresses, and so his supporters came up with a novel plan. They would essentially kidnap all of the pretty girls of Fiume, including D'Annunzio's current lover, and imprison them in a wooden 'castle', where they would not be released until the men arrived with food, money, and gifts - in other words, the products of actual work.

D'Annunzio was a fascinating character, who lived a bizarre and varied life. He was born in Italy, and first found fame as a poet, after publishing his first volume at the age of sixteen. As his fame grew, he produced novels, plays, and operas, but critics began to turn against the perversion and sensuality of his work, regarding him as dangerously amoral. During World War One, he became a daredevil fighter pilot, whose thrilling adventures included a 700-mile round trip to drop propaganda leaflets over Vienna. The leaflets were covered red, white, and green, the colours of the Italian flag, and

carried the simple message, 'Viennese, we could now be drop-
ping bombs on you. Instead we drop a salute.' At the age of
52, he charged the Austrian trenches, carrying a pistol in each
hand, a dagger between his teeth, with his long cloak flapping
behind him.

After the end of World War One, there were many ter-
ritorial questions to be resolved, one of which was what to
do with Fiume. Fiume was a city state close to the borders
of Italy, Austria, Hungary, and Yugoslavia. It had an international population, with three official languages, and occupied
a significant position as a potential buffer between rival states.
Italy was keen to take ownership of Fiume, as was Yugoslavia,
and there were also plans to turn it into an independent state,
or possibly even the home of the new League of Nations.

However, before this issue could be resolved by sensible
diplomacy, the issue was forced by Gabriele D'Annunzio, who
decided to invade on 12 September 1919, along with an army
of 2,000 Fascist followers. He declared an independent state,
under the name the Italian Regency of Carnaro, and named
himself 'Il Duce', in a prototype Fascist government. Thousands of young Italians flocked to Fiume, and the city soon
descended into a chaotic scene of drugs, criminality, and free
love. D'Annunzio's blackshirts swaggered around the streets,
but there was no meaningful order, as inflation soared, food
ran out, and the city's drains became blocked.

The major European powers had no intention of allowing
this situation to continue, and so on 12 November 1920 the
Treaty of Rapallo was signed, under which Italy and Serbia
agreed that Fiume would become an independent Free State,
which meant that D'Annunzio would be removed, so that
elections could be held. During the Christmas of 1920, the
Italian Army and Navy moved in, and D'Annunzio and his

army were quickly defeated. Over the next few years, the Free State of Fiume endured a series of unstable governments and military coups, until in 1924 it was decisively annexed by Italy under another Fascist leader, Benito Mussolini. Today the city is known as Rijeka, and it is located within Croatia.

Some of D'Annunzio's poetry is still popular in Italy today, but his enduring legacy is not his writing, but his influence on Fascism. Over the course of his brief reign, D'Annunzio essentially established the blueprint for Fascism, which would be rigorously copied by those who followed him, in particular Mussolini and Hitler. He instigated the rituals of the balcony address, the Roman salute, the parading of an army of black-shirted followers, and the cries of 'Eia, eia, eia! Alala!', which he claimed were the words shouted by Achilles to speed the horses of his chariot. He was also thought to have instigated the brutal practice of forcing opponents to drink castor oil, which has an unpleasant and humiliating laxative effect. Mussolini felt threatened by D'Annunzio throughout his reign, and essentially paid him off to keep him out of politics. Mussolini explained, 'When you have a rotten tooth you have two possibilities open to you: either you pull the tooth or you fill it with gold. With D'Annunzio I have chosen the latter treatment.'

Where did Edward VIII meet Wallis Simpson?

On 11 December 1936 King Edward VIII abdicated the British throne, stating that he could no longer fulfil his duties without the support of 'the woman I love', meaning of course American divorcée Wallis Simpson. Edward had been essentially forced into choosing between the crown and marriage to Simpson by the parliaments of the constituent nations of the Commonwealth, whose leaders had a range of objections to the marriage. As a result, Edward chose to abdicate, and the crown passed to his younger brother, the stuttering Bertie (recently portrayed by Colin Firth in the Oscar-winning film *The King's Speech*), who became King George VI. Edward was given the title His Royal Highness the Duke of Windsor, and after the marriage, Wallis Simpson became the Duchess of Windsor. However, Simpson was not granted an 'HRH' of her own, and this was a snub which the couple bitterly resented.

So what were the objections? Firstly, as king, Edward was the Supreme Governor of the Church of England, which did not allow divorced people to marry in church. He was also the head of a number of Commonwealth nations with significant Catholic populations, who did not recognise divorce at all. Just as importantly, many of the great and good simply didn't approve of Wallis Simpson. She was felt to have some kind of sexual hold over Edward, and to be using this to exploit him for money and jewels. She was also believed to have been conducting a number of simultaneous affairs, with the Duke of Leinster, and Ford mechanic Guy Trundle.

To many people, the idea of the handsome, charming young King giving up his crown for any woman, let alone a middle-aged American divorcée who was not even particularly beautiful, seemed unthinkable. No English king had ever voluntarily given up the throne. The idea seemed astonishing, which may explain why a range of wild stories began to circulate about Mrs Simpson. It was said that Edward had met her in a Hong Kong brothel, where she had put on lesbian sex shows, and learned exotic Eastern sexual techniques which had cured the prince's premature ejaculation. Others speculated that their relationship was based on sado-masochistic sex, a rumour fuelled by reports of Edward's childish, subservient manner towards her. Another rumour claimed that she was a hermaphrodite, and that Edward found this particularly erotic. In Shangai she was said to have been involved in illegal gambling and the opium trade, as well as indulging in the drug herself, and posing for nude postcards.

There were also a range of more serious claims. UK intelligence services were believed to have compiled a 'China Dossier' on Simpson, which not only contained details of her lurid sexual history, but also suggested that she might have actually been a spy for the US, the Soviet Union, and/or Nazi Germany. The FBI were made aware of allegations that another of Simpson's lovers, at the same time as Edward, was German ambassador Joachim von Ribbentrop, who sent her 17 carnations every day, one for every time they had slept together.

At this distance, it may be impossible to sort the facts from the fiction about Wallis Simpson, but the stories of her 'sexual powers' do seem to have been exaggerated, if not simply invented. There is no record of anyone actually seeing the famous 'China Dossier', and Simpson's more restrained biographers tend to present her time in China as a far more sad, mundane tale than the exotic fantasies of her enemies. Simpson's first husband, American naval pilot Win Spencer, had been a violent drunk, who subjected her to years of abuse. For much of their marriage he was away on naval duties, and she enjoyed a series of affairs. When they attempted a reconciliation in Hong Kong, Spencer made her accompany him to brothels, forcing her to watch as he kissed and groped the working girls.

Wallis Simpson may not have deserved her reputation as an amoral seductress, but her life was far from spotless. During World War Two, the couple were accused of being Nazi sympathisers, a view which the Duke seems to have done little to dispel. He was reported to have said, 'After the war is over and Hitler will crush the Americans... we'll take over... They don't want me as their king, but I'll soon be back as their leader.' The Duchess was suspected of being a Nazi agent, who passed details of the French and Belgian defences to the Germans, facilitating Germany's invasion of Northern France in 1940. When George VI died in 1952, the Duchess refused to accompany her husband to England for the funeral. Still bitter at her treatment by the British establishment, on her last visit she had told the Duke, 'I hate this country. I shall hate it to my grave.'

4

CRUEL CHRONICLES

'The effects of human wickedness are written on the page
of history in characters of blood: but the impression soon
fades away; so more blood must be shed to renew it.'
Guesses at Truth, by Two Brothers, Augustus William Hare
(1792-1834) and Julius Charles Hare (1795-1855)

What was unusual about the way Sparta raised its children?

I imagine your first thought might be to wonder why the
question is phrased in such a strange way. Sparta's children? Don't children belong to their parents, if they belong
to anyone at all? In Sparta, things were different. Sparta was
the archetypal military state, which focused all of its energies
on producing the world's most effective army, and this meant
that all of its citizens, from birth, were seen to belong to the
state. As a result, these children were raised and educated in a
very unusual way, as we shall see.

The reason why Sparta created such a militarily focused
society may be traced to the 8th century BC, when the Spartans crossed the Taygetus mountains and conquered the

neighbouring territory of Messenia. The Spartans now controlled a large territory, but they were heavily outnumbered by the defeated Messenian population, by around ten to one, which meant there was a constant danger of revolt. In 640 BC, the Messenians did revolt, and although Sparta eventually triumphed, it was a close call. To protect itself, Sparta developed a new model of society, which was divided into three classes. Spartans who could trace their ancestry back many generations were deemed *Spartiates*, meaning citizens, and were thus required to serve as full-time soldiers. There was also a middle class, the *perioeci*, which was made up of foreigners and tradesmen, and these were also free men. At the bottom of the pile were the *helots*, the slaves, who made up the majority of the population, and did most of the work. The Spartan system was thus designed to keep the helots under control, and to defend Sparta from attack by its neighbours.

In this military state, there was no place for the weak. As soon as a baby was born, it would be dipped in a bath of wine, to test its strength. A weak child, according to the theory, would convulse and die. If the child survived this first test, it was then taken for inspection by the elders, who would decide whether or not the child was strong enough to become a Spartan. If the baby was thought to be weak or frail in some way, it was taken to the *Apothetae*, a chasm on Mount Taygetos, and left there to die.

Any boy who survived these tests would then spend seven years being raised by his mother, before being removed by the state, to begin his military education. This education, which was called *Agoge*, was designed to toughen him up, and prepare him for warfare. As well as being taught to fight, boys were forced to sleep in the open air, to march without shoes, and to wear a single garment for an entire year. They endured frequent whippings and beatings, and were taught never to show pain or weakness. They were deliberately underfed, to encourage them to learn to steal food stealthily, and live on their wits.

Alongside their military training, boys were also taught to read and write, and encouraged to express themselves with brevity and wit. Sparta is situated in the region of Laconia, and it is from the Spartans that we get the word 'laconic', which sums up the Spartan ideal. On one famous occasion, the Spartans were sent a warning by the great general Philip II of Macedon, stating 'You are advised to submit without further delay, for if I bring my army into your land, I will destroy your farms, slay your people, and raze your city.' The Spartan reply was the definition of laconic: 'If'. Philip never did attack Sparta, and nor did his son, Alexander the Great.

At the age of 16, the boys entered a new stage of their training, known as the *krypteia*, meaning 'secret thing'. They were sent out into the woods, armed only with a knife, and their mission was essentially to wage war against the slave population, killing any helots they could find. This not only trained the boys in warfare and stealth, it also helped to keep the helot population in check. During the same period, the boys would be paired with an older, male mentor, to form a 'relationship'. Accounts of these relationships tend to be euphemistic, but it seems likely that they were to some extent sexual.

At 20, the young men were put through a rigorous test, to determine which candidates were tough enough to become soldiers, and thus citizens. Those who failed would be dumped into the perioeci class, and have to work for a living. Soldiers, on the other hand, would be given land of their own, which would be farmed and managed by the helots, to provide a steady income, while the soldiers themselves continued to live in barracks with their comrades. Even if a soldier chose to marry at this point, he was not allowed to live with his family until the age of thirty, so relationships with women were closely restricted.

The Spartan system was enormously successful, and the small city state grew to become the leading military power in Greece for around 300 years, between the 7th and 4th century BC. Sparta's chief rival was the democratic, cultured city of Athens, which Sparta defeated in the Peloponnesian War of 431-404 BC. However this proved to be a costly victory, and Sparta was soon defeated by Thebes in 371 BC, after which it never regained its former power. Sparta's decline was partly caused by its strict rules regarding citizenship, which could only be inherited by blood, which meant that there was no way to replace those lost in battle. At the beginning of the 5th century BC Sparta's citizen population was around 10,000, but after defeat by Thebes it was less than 1,000. As a result, the citizens became even more dramatically outnumbered by the helots, and slave revolts became increasingly threatening. Sparta was eventually conquered at the start of the 2nd century BC, and forced to join the Achaean league, a confederation of Greek city states.

What was the Roman Emperor Elagabalus's strange idea of a practical joke?

Elagabalus reigned as Roman Emperor from 218-222 AD, and he is generally regarded as having been one of the very worst of all Rome's emperors, whose tenure was symptomatic of the decadence and depravity that marked the last centuries of the Empire, leading to its eventual collapse. One of the Emperor's favourite pranks was to get his guests so drunk that they collapsed in a stupor. He would then have his servants lock them in the hall, before leading in his menagerie of lions, leopards, and bears. When the groggy guests awoke, they would find themselves surrounded by a terrifying array of deadly predators, the sight of which alone was enough to scare of them some to death. The animals were apparently tame, and possibly declawed and defanged, so the threat they posed may have been to some extent limited, but of course the guests didn't know this, and it's hard to imagine just how terrifying an experience this must have been.

As you may have guessed, Elagabalus was a young man, with a young man's sense of humour. He was installed as emperor at the age of just 14, thanks to the machinations of his mother and grandmother, who claimed he was the illegitimate child of the last emperor but one, Caracalla, although there seems to have been no truth to this claim. If Elagabalus's mother and grandmother assumed he would be a puppet they could control, they were soon disabused of this error, as the young emperor demonstrated that control and restraint would play no part at his court.

His pranks and cruelty were shameful, but they were far less significant than his contempt for the traditions and culture of Rome. Elagabalus was a Syrian, who quickly filled his court with unqualified countrymen, and insisted that Romans would now follow the Syrian god El-Gabal. Rome's most respected citizens were forced to worship the 'Black Stone', the most sacred object of Elagabalus's cult (it was probably a meteorite). Cattle and sheep were sacrificed daily, and there were stories of genital mutilation, and the sacrifice of young children, although any stories regarding Elagabalus have to be taken with a pinch of salt, as many sources lie somewhere between exaggeration and outright fiction. Elagabalus even announced that he had married a Vestal Virgin, trampling all over a sacred tradition that was almost a thousand years old which held that any Vestal Virgin who engaged in sex would immediately suffer execution, along with her lover.

Elagabalus then quickly abandoned this marriage, which was one of at least five he undertook during his short life, although he seems to have been predominantly homosexual. He was believed to have had numerous male lovers, including a blond Greek slave named Hierocles whom he described as his husband. Elagabalus would parade around his palace naked, and prostitute himself in the taverns and brothels of Rome. Sometimes he arranged for Hierocles to catch him in the act, resulting in his 'husband' punishing him with a beating. Elagabalus may well have been what we would call transgender or transsexual today, as he shaved his body hair, wore make-up, and presented himself as a woman. He even offered a huge reward to any doctor who could successfully operate on him to turn him into a woman.

As you might imagine, this teenage libertine was not a popular Emperor. His position was entirely dependent upon the support of the army, which was founded only on their loyalty to his supposed ancestor, Caracalla. However, the army's patience was limited. After Elagabalus made the mistake of announcing an heir, the Praetorian Guard now had a focus for their opposition, and soon set upon Elagabalus and his mother, and beheaded them both, before throwing their bodies into the river Tiber.

Why did slaves have cause to thank the Roman Emperor Constantine?

The Roman Emperor Constantine is generally known by the honorific 'Constantine The Great', and his reign was undoubtedly a long and successful one, lasting more than thirty years from 306-337 AD. Constantine was the first Roman Emperor to be a Christian, and a key figure in the spread and growth of the religion. He won numerous military victories, including successes against the Franks, Visigoths, and Alamanni. He united the fractured Roman Empire under a single leader, and effectively founded what has come to be known as the Byzantine Empire, when he moved the capital east to Byzantium, which became known as Constantinople. His enduring reputation was demonstrated by the fact that ten future Byzantine emperors, including the very last, would take the name 'Constantine'.

As the first Christian emperor, Constantine made a number of laws which improved conditions for slaves. He banned crucifixion and branding on the face as punishments. Before this, a slave who had tried to escape would have the letters 'FUG' branded onto their forehead, which was short for the Latin word *fugitivus*, meaning 'runaway'. Gladiatorial games were banned, and prisoners were no longer to be kept in total darkness, but instead were given time outdoors, in daylight.

So should we consider Constantine to have been a kind, benevolent leader, who eschewed draconian punishments? Well, not quite. Constantine only disapproved of branding on the face because of a contemporary Christian belief that the face had a special religious significance; branding anywhere else was still fine. Similarly, crucifixion was banned only because of its association with Christ, but slaves could still be forced to drink boiling oil or molten lead. Slave owners under Constantine were still allowed to beat their slaves to death, or to amputate their feet if they tried to escape. Constantine had no problem with cruel punishments – criminals could still have their eyes gouged out, or their legs cut off – and he was particularly harsh when it came to sexual morality. Parents who failed to prevent their daughters from 'being seduced' were to be punished by having molten lead poured down their throat.

A lack of sexual morality was to cause one of the most dramatic scandals of the Emperor's own life. In the year 326, Constantine had his eldest son Crispus executed by 'cold poison', apparently for having had sexual relations with Constantine's second wife, the Empress Fausta, who was Crispus's stepmother. Fausta died soon afterwards, of suffocation in an over-heated bath, presumably killed on Constantine's orders. Constantine then ordered that the lives of Crispus and Fausta should be stricken from the records, and so as a result the pair are barely mentioned in any ancient sources.

We do have one thing to thank Constantine for, as it was arguably he who invented the weekend. Before Constantine, some Romans still observed an eight-day week, but Constantine issued an edict establishing that a week should have seven days, and that one of these, Sunday, should be the day of rest, when no trade was to be allowed. Thus, thanks to the Emperor, people finally started to get a day off work. No wonder they called him Constantine The Great.

How did the Carolingian leader Carloman address the problem of rebellious Alamanni nobles?

Carloman was one of the heirs of the Carolingian Empire, which covered almost all of Western Europe north of the Pyrenees. This region is usually described as the Frankish Realm or Frankish Kingdoms. The region had been solely ruled by Carloman's father, Charles Martel, who was effectively the king, although he chose not to use this title. When

Charles died, Carloman and his brother Pippin chose to share power, having ousted their other brother, Grifo. They decided that Pippin would rule Neustria in the west, which is roughly the area of France today, while Carloman would rule Austrasia in the east, which is broadly modern-day Germany. This arrangement was surprisingly successful, as the two brothers supported each other in military action, while each had their own base of power and wealth.

Carloman appears to have been one of the most pious rulers of the age. He set up the first major synod to take place in Austrasia, the *Concilium Germanicum*, and chaired it himself. While Charles Martel had taken wealth out of the church to fund his military campaigns, Carloman instead gave money and land to the church, and funded the building of new churches. Of course, historically many leaders have seen the good political sense in harnessing the support of the clergy, but Carloman seems rather to have acted out of sincere, deeply held religious beliefs. Amazingly, in 747 he retired from kingship, to join a monastery in Rome. He later founded a monastery at Monte Soratte, after which he travelled to Monte Cassino, where he spent most of the remainder of his life, with one significant exception. In 754, he was asked by Pope Stephen II to meet with Pippin, to ask him not to invade Italy. Carloman carried out this request, but Pippin refused to give the desired assurance, and instead imprisoned Carloman, who died soon afterwads.

So, to return to the question, how did this unusually pious man deal with his political opponents? The opponents in question were the nobles of the Alamannia region, around the upper reaches of the river Rhine, who had carried out a series of armed rebellions against Carloman. In response, in 746 Carloman called the nobles to an assembly at Cannstatt, present-day Stuttgart. Thousands of Alamanni magnates arrived, and soon found themselves arrested. Then, Carloman simply had all of them executed for treason, in what has become known as the Blood Court at Canstatt. With this one brutal action, Carloman effectively wiped out the entire class of Alamanni nobles. He then simply replaced them with his own Frankish appointees, and thus ended the problem of Alamanni resistance at one (ruthless) fell swoop.

Was Edward II killed as a result of a misplaced comma?

Edward II of England reigned from 1307 to 1327, but his was a miserable and bloody reign, and he is consequently regarded as having been one of England's very worst monarchs. He was born in 1284, the fourth son of the popular Edward I, who had been both an effective administrator and a leading general, whose military triumphs included the conquest of Wales. Edward I died in July 1307, having outlived his three eldest sons, and so Edward II was crowned. However, the new king seems to have lacked the strength and authority of his father, being generally described as extravagant and frivolous, and his reign faced opposition from the start.

One of Edward's first acts was to recall Piers Gaveston from exile. Gaveston was a young Gascon knight who had been banished to France by Edward I, because he was felt to be a bad influence on the young prince. Now that he was free to lavish gifts upon his friend, Edward II gave Gaveston the earldom of Cornwall, a title which had previously only been conferred on royalty. This upset the barons, who became increasingly concerned at Gaveston's influence on the young king. It was widely believed that Edward and Gaveston were lovers, with a number of contemporary sources criticising Edward for his desire for 'wicked and forbidden sex', while another stated that 'Edward took too much delight in sodomy'. In 1310 and 1311 Parliament imposed restrictions on Edward's power, and forced Gaveston into exile. In 1312, the barons rebelled again, murdering Gaveston, and forcing Edward to accept further limitations to his powers.

By 1314, Edward had been losing ground for seven years in the ongoing war with Scotland. He was now in danger of losing the crucial stronghold of Stirling Castle, and so he raised an enormous army of 20,000 foot soldiers and 3,000 cavalrymen, and prepared to meet Robert the Bruce at Bannockburn. However, despite Edward's huge numerical advantage, he was tactically outthought, allowing Bruce to choose the field of battle that would best suit the Scots' forces. With his army defeated, Edward's grip on power disintegrated, and his cousin Thomas of Lancaster became king in all but name. However, Lancaster seems to have been as hapless as Edward himself, and by 1318 the pair were reconciled, and ruling jointly.

Edward now had two new favourites, Hugh le Despenser and his son, who confusingly was also called Hugh. As before, Edward began lavishing wealth and influence on his pets, upsetting the nobility in the process. When he handed the Despensers ownership of the Welsh peninsula of Gower, despite them having no legal claim to it, the barons (led by Lancaster) revolted, and forced the Despensers into exile. Edward fought back, and defeated Lancaster in battle at Boroughbridge in March 1322, before executing him, and recalling the Despensers. Edward now began a bloody campaign against his enemies, executing 28 knights and barons who had opposed him, and exiling many others.

In 1325, opposition to Edward began to form around his wife Isabella of France. Edward sent her to France on a diplomatic mission, where she became the mistress of Roger Mortimer, one of Edward's exiled enemies. When Edward foolishly sent his son to join her, she now had control of the heir apparent. In September 1326, Isabella and Mortimer invaded England. They had only a tiny army, but it was more than adequate, as Edward was unable to raise an army of his own, and so they faced no resistance. Edward was captured and forced to abdicate, while the Despensers were brutally executed. Despenser the Younger was publicly hanged, castrated, and then drawn and quartered. On 25 January 1327, Edward's 14 year old son was proclaimed King Edward III. Later that year, Edward II was murdered at Berkeley Castle in Gloucestershire, reportedly by having a red hot poker thrust into his anus.

So, you may be wondering, what does this have to do with a misplaced comma? The answer is that there is a long-standing story that Isabella and Mortimer tried to cover their tracks when giving the order for Edward's murder, by sending the Latin message, 'Eduardum occidere nolite timere bonum est', which can be read in two very distinct ways. If a comma is understood to come after the word 'timere', the message reads, 'Do not be afraid to kill Edward; it is good.' If, however, the phrasing is assumed to include a comma before 'timere', the message is the very different, 'Do not kill Edward; it is good to fear.' In this way, the pair could issue an instruction which was both as explicit as it needed to be, but also deniable.

What was the Aztecs' unusual method for choosing a king?

The Aztec society of 14th-16th century Mesoamerica had a very unusual method of selecting a king. Once a year, during the 20-day month of Toxcatl, the most handsome man would be selected from among the Aztecs' captured prisoners of war, and he would be made king for a year. A year later, he would be ritually sacrificed, in tribute to the Aztecs' most powerful god, Tezcatlipoca.

Human sacrifice was an important feature of the Aztecs' shocking, blood-soaked culture. The Aztecs believed that their gods had sacrificed themselves for humankind's sake, and that the only way to renew and sustain life and the earth's resources was through an ongoing cycle of human sacrifice. Sacrifice was therefore seen as a necessary form of public service, which was described by the word *nextlahualli*, which can be roughly translated as 'payment of debt'.

The Aztecs also believed that the way in which a person died was the key factor in determining which of the levels of the afterlife they would be transported to. If a person died peacefully at home, this meant that they would travel to the very lowest level of the afterlife, where they would undergo a whole range of unpleasant tortures and ordeals, before ending up in a grim underworld. A 'good' death, on the other hand, was considered to be one that resulted from human sacrifice, war, or childbirth. People who died in these ways were known as the *Teo-micqui*, meaning 'God-dead', and were believed to go to the second-highest level of heaven (the very highest was reserved for children who died in infancy).

Consequently, human sacrifice seems to have been seen as an honour to be sought, rather than a fate to be avoided. Although there are records of sacrifice victims losing their nerve, crying, or losing control of their bowels, this seems to have been unusual enough to have been remarkable. The Spanish conquistadores Cortes and Alvarado were Christians, who were horrified by the human sacrifices, but they found that when they tried to rescue the intended victims, they would protest angrily, demanding to be allowed to be sacrificed. Sacrifices were often the culmination of an elaborate day of rituals, with the victim taking an active, central role in the celebrations. This adds to the impression that the victims were often willing and compliant, as many of the festivities described could only have taken place with the active participation of the victims.

It was therefore a great honour to be chosen to represent Tezcatlipoca for a year, as the new king would be treated like a god on earth, with people kissing the ground as he passed. He would be indulged and spoiled in every way, protected by armed guards, dressed in the most luxurious robes, and entertained by four attractive courtesans. He would also be taught to sing, dance, and play the flute.

At the end of the year, the king would lead a parade, attended by his concubines, before being led to the top of the temple pyramid, and stripped naked. His body would then be stretched out on a sacrificial altar, and his torso sliced open. The high priests would now tear out his still-beating heart, and raise it in the air, as an offering to the gods. The king's head would now be impaled on a pole, while his skin was flayed from his body, before being draped on the shoulders of a high priest, like a gruesome, bloody cloak.

What was the unpleasant fate of Hungarian revolutionary György Dózsa?

At the start of the 16th century, Hungary was one of leading powers in Europe, but its leader, Cardinal Tamás Bakócz, could see trouble on the horizon. Since the fall of the Byzantine Empire, Hungary had been Christianity's first line of defence against the Turkish Empire. Turkey was currently weak, but growing in strength. Bakócz concluded that he should strike now, from a position of strength, rather than waiting for Turkey to become a significant threat.

The Hungarian nobility had no interest in starting an unnecessary and expensive war, so Bakócz came up with a different solution: a crusade. A crusade would not need the support of the nobility, as it would be made up of serfs. Serfdom in Hungary at this time was effectively a form of slavery, as any serf who attempted to leave his master's estate would be hunted down, and he and his family would be tortured. A crusade offered an opportunity for serfs to leave this life of pain and toil, and possibly win themselves the right to spend the afterlife in heaven, not to mention the possibility of loot in this life. On April 16, 1514 Bakócz succeeded in persuading Pope Leo X to issue a papal bull declaring a Holy War against the Turks, which would be commanded by György Dózsa, a proven military leader. Within a short time, more than 100,000 so-called *Kurucs* had joined up.

There were just two problems. Firstly, while the Cardinal was planning his crusade, the King of Hungary decided to agree a wide-ranging peace and trade treaty with Turkey. Secondly, with many of the strongest and healthiest peasants signing up for the crusade, the nobility's estates were being neglected, with crops left rotting in the fields, and soon there was widespread famine. The nobles became increasingly aggressive in their efforts to intimidate and coerce the serfs back to work, and so eventually the papal bull was rescinded, and the crusade was officially cancelled.

However, György Dózsa had other ideas. At this point, Dózsa and the other crusade leaders decided on a new agenda, which was essentially a socialist revolution, to improve the conditions of life for the workers, and remove the privileges enjoyed by the nobility. Dózsa demanded that all of Hungary's land was to be divided among the poor, and all the people were now to considered equal in the eyes of the law. The revolution began, as nobles were slaughtered, monasteries and manor houses were sacked, and fields were burned. Any nobles who resisted were killed with appalling cruelty, which included crucifixion, torture, and impalement. The Hungarian authorities attempted to send the cavalry out of the towns to quell the revolutionaries, but they were attacked and unhorsed before they could even make it out of the town gates, as even the non-crusading peasants rose up and joined the violence. For weeks, Hungary descended into anarchy.

The Hungarian social order seemed to be on the brink of collapse, as Dózsa's army managed to equip themselves with cannons and trained gunners. However, despite their numerical strength, the revolutionaries were mostly untrained, malnourished peasants. The King hired mercenaries from Bohemia, Venice and the Holy Roman Empire, and put together an organised, well-armed force of 20,000 men. Soon, their superior training and equipment began to tell, and the *Kurucs* were crushed.

Any revolutionaries who were captured were now tortured or killed, but a special punishment was reserved for Dózsa. He was forced to sit, practically naked, on a red-hot throne made of iron, holding a red-hot sceptre, as a red-hot crown was placed on his head, in mockery of his perceived ambitions of kingship. Nine of the revolutionaries were led in, having been starved for three days. The guards now gouged chunks from the still-conscious Dózsa's body using red-hot pliers, and threw them to his former supporters, who were forced to eat their leader's flesh.

Not only did this mark one of the most barbaric episodes in European history, it was also politically disastrous. Around 70,000 nobles and serfs had been killed, and the economy was close to collapse. The resurgent Turkish Empire was now perfectly placed to capitalise on Hungary's weakness and social divisions. In 1526, the Ottoman Turks successfully invaded, and this invasion was partly achieved through the invaders' success in presenting themselves as the saviours of the downtrodden Hungarian serfs. Centuries later, Dózsa became an iconic figure for the new Communist states of Eastern Europe, and many streets in Hungary and Romania still bear his name.

Who was the 'Wrath Of God'?

The answer is the Spanish conquistadore Lope de Aguirre, who remains a figure of enduring fascination as a result of his astonishingly cruel and vengeful nature. He was born into the nobility in northern Spain, in around the year 1510. When Aguirre was in his twenties, the explorer Hernándo Pizarro returned to Spain from Peru, having become fabulously wealthy, after capturing the treasures of the Incas. Inspired by Pizarro's example, Aguirre enlisted in an expedition, arriving in Peru in around 1536-7.

Aguirre's evil character may have been moulded in 1548, when he was working as a soldier guarding the Potosí silver mines. Aguirre and a number of the troops were charged with mistreating the local natives, by making them carrying the Spaniards' baggage. This was a fairly minor offence, but the judge in charge, Francisco de Esquivel, decided to make an example of Aguirre, and sentenced him to 200 lashes. This was seen as a major humiliation for a Spaniard to be flogged in front of the natives, let alone one of noble birth such as

Aguirre. He pleaded that he would rather die than submit to such a disgrace, but his protests were ignored, and he was forced to endure his punishment.

After this, Aguirre's shame was all-consuming. He refused to wear shoes or ride a horse, stating that he was not worthy of them. Instead, he vowed revenge on Esquivel, and pursued him on foot for three years. The judge, scared for his life, fled from city to city, but Aguirre was relentless, chasing him barefoot for 6,000 kilometres over the course of three years. He eventually caught up with Esquivel in Cuzco, Peru, where he found him asleep, wearing a coat of chainmail, which he wore constantly out of fear. Aguirre now had his revenge, killing Esquivel by stabbing him in the head, before escaping in disguise.

After gaining his revenge, Aguirre seems to have disappeared for close to a decade, presumably because he needed to lay low, having just killed a judge. He reappeared in 1560, to join a new expedition led by Pedro de Ursúa. The expedition was a quest for the site of El Dorado, the mythical land of unlimited gold, which a group of natives claimed they had found deep in the Amazon rainforest in Brazil. The Spanish had carried out a number of expeditions in their quest for El Dorado, and so this trip might have been fairly unremarkable, had it not been for the presence of Lope de Aguirre. The party included around 370 Spanish soldiers, along with thousands of Peruvian natives. The Spanish party was comprised of criminals, pirates, and other rebels, whom the Spanish authorities were keen to get rid of, which perhaps explains Aguirre's reappearance at this point.

In September 1560, the expedition set off down a tributary of the Amazon, on a flotilla of rafts, boats, and canoes. Ursúa was quickly revealed to be a weak leader, who alien-

ated his men by bringing along his beautiful girlfriend, Inez de
Atienza. Once the expedition reached the rainforest, all discipline collapsed, and the soldiers began massacring any natives
they encountered, as well as fighting among themselves. Disorder soon led to outright mutiny, and Ursúa was murdered.
He was replaced by a Spanish nobleman, Don Fernando de
Guzmán, but he was merely a puppet, as the real leader was
now Lope de Aguirre. The rabble now abandoned their pursuit of El Dorado for a new goal, which was no less than
the invasion and capture of Peru. Under Aguirre's influence,
Guzmán agreed to issue a direct challenge to the Spanish
Viceroy, declaring himself 'Lord and Prince of Peru'. In the
document announcing their intentions, many of the rebels
sought to justify and mitigate their treacherous actions, but
Aguirre simply signed his name: 'Aguirre – Traitor'.

The journey that followed was one of unremitting horror
and carnage. Guzmán was soon killed, along with Inez, who
had transferred her affections to him, and they were soon
joined by anyone who had shown loyalty to Guzmán. The
site of these savage killings became known as the 'town of
the butchery'. Aguirre now openly took control, as the army
drove on towards the sea, destroying any native villages they
encountered on the way. Over the course of this journey,
the increasingly paranoid Aguirre would order the killing of
anyone he suspected of disloyalty, and all it would take to raise
his suspicions would be for a group of soldiers to be seen talking together. Murder became an everyday occurrence. At one
point, Aguirre turned on the natives in the party, and left them
stranded on an island in the middle of the Amazon. These
natives were Christians from Peru, for whom the Amazon
rainforest was just as dangerous and terrifying as it was to
the Spanish. By the summer of 1561 Aguirre had killed more

than 140 of the Spaniards, from a party which had comprised just 370 at the start.

In July 1561 Aguirre and his army successfully invaded the island of Margarita, off the coast of Venezuela, before landing in Peru. Aguirre declared, 'I am the Wrath of God, the Prince of Freedom, Lord of Tierra Firme and the Provinces of Chile.' However, the Spanish troops were now closing in, and Aguirre's army was rapidly shrinking. He now killed his daughter Elvira, claiming that this was to prevent her from being captured, 'because someone that I loved so much should not come to be bedded by uncouth people.' Eventually he was killed by his own men, who shot him in the chest, before beheading and quartering the corpse.

Who was the Blood Countess?

This was one of the nicknames given to the notorious Hungarian countess Elizabeth Báthory, who may have been the most prolific female serial killer in history. Báthory's astonishing catalogue of murder and torture is such that many believe that it was she, as much as the more commonly cited Vlad Dracula (also known as Vlad the Impaler), who was the inspiration for Bram Stoker's gothic horror novel *Dracula*.

During Báthory's early life, there were few signs of the horrors to come. She was born in Hungary in 1560 into the influential Báthory family, whose lands and titles included the princedom of Transylvania. Elizabeth's parents were cousins, as was common practice at the time among the European nobility, but this inbreeding may have been the source of her insanity, as she is believed to have suffered from seizures and epilepsy from childhood. Even so, Elizabeth was said to have been a great beauty, as well as being a well educated young woman, who spoke four languages, and studied astronomy and science. In 1575 she married Ferenc Nádasdy, in a lavish ceremony at the palace of Varannó with 4,500 guests.

Life was cheap in 16th century Hungary, particularly the life of a serf. While Báthory's husband was away leading the Hungarian army in the Long War against the Ottoman Empire, Elizabeth was responsible for defending and managing their lands. This would routinely involve a certain level of brutality towards the peasantry, but her husband is believed to have cultivated a reputation as an unusually harsh master.

From 1602 onwards, rumours and allegations began to circulate about horrendous crimes and witchcraft taking place at Báthory's Csejte Castle. Báthory was said to be sexually involved with her female servants, some of whom were witches, who aided their mistress in her sadistic entertainment. The Hungarian King Matthias eventually called for an investigation, and so a number of Báthory's servants were arrested and put on trial, while Báthory herself was kept under house arrest. According to reports, a number of young girls were found dead or imprisoned in the castle on the day the arrests were made.

Over the course of the investigation, more than 300 witnesses testified, describing an enormous catalogue of crimes committed by Báthory and her servants. Young peasant girls had been abducted, or lured to the castle by offers of work, and then brutally beaten, burned, frozen, sexually assaulted, and tortured. One account described a kind of woman-shaped metal cage, known as the 'Iron Virgin' into which the victim would be locked, before a wall of spikes or blades was thrust into the cage. Another account described Báthory savagely biting her victims, tearing into their flesh with her teeth. One of the most famous details of the Blood Countess's reign of terror concerns her literal blood-baths, as she would bathe in the blood of her young victims, as well as drinking it, to preserve her youth and beauty. According to the legend, this practice began after Báthory observed that her skin felt tighter after a beaten servant's blood splashed onto her face.

At the conclusion of the trial, four of Báthory's servants were put to death, with three of them first having their fingers ripped off with hot pliers, before being burned at the stake. The fourth servant, who was believed to have taken a less prominent role in the tortures, was merely beheaded, before being burned at the stake. Accounts of the number of the victims varied enormously, with one servant claiming that Báthory had kept a journal listing as many as 650 victims.

However, many of the accounts of Báthory's crimes are unreliable, for a number of reasons. Firstly, the confessions were all extracted under torture, or the threat of torture, and as a result many of them are extremely sensational and inconsistent. Secondly, historians have further clouded the picture by adding further lurid details with each retelling. For example, the story of Báthory bathing in the blood of her victims doesn't appear in any of the contemporary accounts; in fact, it doesn't seem to have been introduced into the legend until 1729, when the Jesuit László Turóczi published the first account of the case in his *Tragica Historia*.

The third reason we have to doubt some of the most lurid aspects of the Elizabeth Báthory story is that she herself was never put on trial, charged, or convicted, and her opponents had significant incentives to discredit and damage her. Hungary's King Matthias, who ordered the trial, had run up a significant debt to Báthory, which he was unable to repay. Discrediting and imprisoning her meant he could write off his debt, seize her lands, as well as damaging the power base of the Protestant Báthory family, who posed a threat to the

Catholic Habsburg monarchy to which he belonged. Consequently, it was clearly in Matthias's interests to exaggerate Báthory's crimes.

How did Frederick the Great enforce discipline?

Frederick the Great of Prussia is widely regarded as having been one of the greatest leaders of the 18th century. He reigned for 46 years from 1740-1786, during which time he turned Prussia from a small provincial backwater into one of the leading powers in Europe. He was born in 1712, the son of King Frederick William I of Prussia, who was a strict authoritarian. Frederick William insisted his son's education be purely focused on practical, military training, but Frederick had an artistic spirit, and thanks to his mother managed to gain an education in French, Latin, music and literature. Frederick became a dedicated scholar, an accomplished musician and composer, and an all-round man of letters, who go on would form a lifelong friendship with the great French writer Voltaire. During his teenage years, however, Frederick became increasingly unhappy at the kind of restricted life he was expected to lead, and his relationship with his father deteriorated. Frederick William was prone to violent outbursts, and on occasions he had to be physically separated from his son.

Perhaps the most traumatic event of Frederick's life took place in 1730, when he was just 18. The young prince had often thought of running away, and so on a trip to South Germany with his father, he made a plan to escape to England, to the court of his uncle King George II. Frederick intended to set off with a number of junior army officers, including two friends, Lieutenants Katte and Keith, but Keith lost his nerve, and confessed the plans to King Frederick William. As they were serving members of the military, Frederick and Katte were court martialled and charged with treason, for which the penalty was death. Frederick was spared this punishment (although his father is said to have given it serious consideration), but was forced to watch as his friend Katte was decapitated. For two days afterwards, Frederick suffered from spells of fainting and hallucinations.

After his father's death, Frederick became a much loved king, who was celebrated for his caring nature. He showed great concern for the welfare of his troops, and identified himself as a friend to the poor. He pursued an enlightened approach to government, based on justice, freedom of the press, and religious tolerance. However, although Frederick's instincts were clearly more liberal than those of his father, he was far from naïve, and he understood the critical importance of maintaining discipline in his army, particularly given that Prussia was so much smaller and poorer than her rivals, as well as bearing the significant tactical disadvantage of being surrounded. Thus, he was quick to stamp out any disobedience among his troops, as an unfortunate captain by the name of Zietern learned during the first war of Silesia.

Frederick was keen to make alterations to his camp during the night, without being seen by the enemy, so he ordered that, after a certain hour, no lights or fires could be lit in any of tents, on pain of death. In government, Frederick was a notorious micro-manager, and he took the same approach with his army. That night, he walked through the camp after the appointed hour, to make sure that there were no lights visible. When he reached Captain Zietern's tent, he saw the light from a thin candle burning. He entered the tent, and found Zietern sealing the wax on a letter to his beloved wife. 'What are you doing?' asked Frederick, 'Do you not know the orders?'. Zietern admitted his guilt, and begged on his knees for mercy. Frederick ordered the man to sit up, unseal the letter, and add some words at the end, which Frederick would dictate. Zietern now wrote the following words, as dictated by Frederick: 'Tomorrow I shall perish on the scaffold.' The next day, Captain Zietern was executed, and some time later his wife must have received a very confusing and upsetting letter.

Who is the only known holder of the Victorious Cross?

The answer is the former Ugandan leader Idi Amin, or to give him his full title: His Excellency Field Marshal Al Hadji Doctor, Idi Amin Dada, President for Life, Conqueror of the British Empire in Africa in General and Uganda in Particular, Victorious Cross, Member of the Excellent Order of the Source of the Nile. Most of these were invented titles, of course, which Amin simply awarded to himself, some of which were clearly mischievous parodies of British titles – Amin's 'Victorious Cross' sounds a lot like the Victoria Cross, but otherwise bears no relation to it. Similarly, 'Conqueror of the British Empire' gives the acronym CBE, but has no connection to the British title CBE, which stands for Commander of the British Empire.

Idi Amin's bizarre collection of titles provides a small clue to this dangerous tyrant's unhinged state of mind, as his reign was one of the most barbaric periods of any nation's history. Amin was born some time in the mid-1920s, when Uganda was a British colony. He became a cook in the King's African Rifles, and quickly rose through the ranks. Amin was a natural candidate for promotion. He was six foot four and powerfully built, and was Uganda's light-heavyweight boxing champion for nine years between 1951-60. He was also a formidable rugby player, and was generally perceived by British officers to be loyal but not particularly bright, an ideal combination.

As Britain prepared to return Uganda to independence, it was keen to promote native Ugandans, and so Amin became one of the country's only two black officers. However, there were early signs of Amin's dangerous character. Given a simple assignment to look into cattle rustling in the Turkana region of Kenya, Amin instead led his troops in what became a massacre, with victims being tortured, beaten to death, and buried alive.

After Uganda gained her independence, Amin became the head of the army, under the socialist president Dr Milton Obote. Like so many before him, Obote underestimated Amin. In 1971, Obote arranged for Amin to be arrested following an assassination attempt, but instead Amin instigated a military coup, and Obote was forced into exile. At first, the people were delighted, but soon blood began to flow. In Amin's first year of power, around two thirds of the 9,000-strong army were killed, along with huge numbers of judges, journalists, and other civilians, particularly those from the Acholi and Langi tribes which had supported Obote. Amin also murdered Brigadier Hussein Sulieman, one of his rivals in the military, and is said to have kept Sulieman's head in his fridge.

Amin set up four rival agencies to carry out his killings, mostly operating in plain clothes, creating a climate of terror and lawlessness. Amin liked to be personally involved in the killings, instigating horrific games such as getting prisoners to kill one another with sledgehammers, or finishing them off himself, by stamping on their chests in his heavy army boots. Over the course of Idi Amin's brutal reign, it is estimated that as many as 500,000 Ugandans were killed, out of a population of just 10 million. Amin even found a novel way of paying his killers, by charging the relatives of the victims for the right to collect their bodies for burial.

One possible reason that Amin's reign of terror was allowed to continue for so long was that he had a bizarre sense of humour, which encouraged journalists and diplomats to see him as a relatively harmless buffoon. In one stunt, he arranged for himself to be carried by a retinue of European businessmen, while one held a dainty parasol over Amin's head, in a scene he named 'The White Man's Burden', in a satirical reference to Rudyard Kipling's imperialistic poem of the same name. He invited Britain's defeated Prime Minister Edward Heath to bring his band on a concert tour of Uganda, and offered to pay the now unemployed Heath with chickens and goats. When Britain fell into economic crisis, he started a 'Save Britain Fund', and sent a planeload of vegetables to feed the starving masses. The international community only began to wake up to Amin's real nature in 1973 when he openly praised Adolf Hitler soon after the Munich massacre, declaring, 'Germany is the right place, where, when Hitler was Prime Minister and Supreme Commander, he burnt over six million Jews. This is because Hitler and all the German people know that the Israelis are not people who are working in the interests of the people of the world.'

Like most bullies, Amin did not relish a fair fight. In October 1978, Amin's troops invaded Tanzania, raping and massacring as they advanced. When the well-trained Tanzanians fought back, the Ugandan army soon collapsed into disarray, and Amin fled the country. He escaped to Libya, where he was granted asylum by Colonel Gaddafi, until he tried to take advantage of the Colonel's daughter, and was promptly banished. He ended up in Saudi Arabia, where the ruling family agreed to keep him in luxury, on condition of him remaining incommunicado. The Saudis clearly felt that the best solution to minimise embarrassment for the Muslim world would be to keep Idi Amin in well-fed silence.

5
NOTABLE NOMENCLATURE

'History is the short trudge from Adam to atom.'
Leonard Louis Levinson (1904-1974)

Why was it called a 'Trojan' Horse?

As described in Chapter One, Odysseus's brilliant scheme for infiltrating Troy was conceived by the Greeks, built by the Greeks, and delivered by the Greeks. The wooden horse was filled with Greeks, and it was directly responsible for a wonderful Greek victory, as the Trojans were defeated, and their city destroyed. Given all of this, why on earth do we call it a 'Trojan' Horse?

The answer is that the emblem of the city of Troy was a horse, much as the bald eagle is the emblem of the USA, or the lion is the emblem of Great Britain. The Greeks were thus delivering what was widely understood to be a Trojan Horse, as a symbolic tribute, even though the Trojans had nothing to do with this particular construction, and obviously gained nothing from its existence.

On a similar note, it's also not clear why the beautiful Helen has become known to history as Helen of Troy. As has already been described, Helen was Greek, not Trojan. She was the Queen of Sparta, before being abducted by Paris, prince of Troy. The Greek sources give conflicting accounts of how far this abduction was forced, with some accounts stating that Helen fell in love with Paris. The sources are equally varied on whether or not Helen ever even arrived in Troy, as some versions state that she spent the duration of the war in Egypt. Paris seems to have been an active figure throughout the war, before being killed in the later stages by Philoctetes. Helen then returned to Sparta with her husband, Meneleus. It is perhaps therefore somewhat unfair that Helen, a Greek princess who may never have set foot in Troy, who was quite possibly forcibly abducted by a Trojan prince, has nonetheless been branded with the name Helen of Troy for eternity.

What is a Pyrrhic victory?

A Pyrrhic victory is one which comes at such a great cost that it might as well have been a defeat. The term refers to King Pyrrhus of Epirus, who won a number of notable but costly victories against the Romans during what has become known as the Pyrrhic War. Although the phrase originated in a military context, it can be used in reference to any kind of conflict where the benefits of victory are outweighed by the losses incurred, so it is also applied to expensive legal battles, or ruinous business takeovers.

The phrase is generally thought to refer to Pyrrhus's two victories over the Romans at Heracles in 280 BC and Asculum in 179 BC. In both cases, despite notionally winning the battle, Pyrrhus suffered devastating losses, losing most of his trusted officers and best soldiers, who could only be replaced with substandard Italian mercenaries, whereas the Romans could draw on considerable reserves. At Heracles, Pyrrhus's Epirotes may have lost as many as 13,000 of their army of 25,000 men, with many losses being caused by a stampede of Pyrrhus's own 20 war elephants. The next year, Pyrrhus marched on Rome again, this time with a force of somewhere between 40-70,000 men. The Battle of Asculum lasted two days, and Pyrrhus was again victorious, but again suffered huge losses. After the battle, he is said to have exclaimed, 'Another such victory and we shall be utterly ruined.'

History is littered with other examples of Pyrrhic victories. World War One as a whole is a good example of a Pyrrhic victory, as the European Allies suffered huge losses in terms of human life, infrastructure, and financial costs, for no obvious major gains. Another example of a Pyrrhic victory was the Battle of Guilford Court House in 1781, during the American War of Independence. The battle was fought in North Carolina between 1,900 British troops under Lord Cornwallis, and the American forces led by General Nathaneal Greene. The British technically won the battle, but lost more than a quarter of their men in the process, and as a result this battle is thought to have been decisive in Britain losing control of the South.

Another striking example of a Pyrrhic victory is the Battle of Isandlwana, which was the first major encounter in the Anglo-Zulu war between the Zulu Kingdom and the British Empire. The Zulu forces attacked Britain's small force of around 2,000 men with a large army of 20,000 warriors. Although the Zulus were mainly armed with spears, against the British rifles and artillery, their numerical superiority was such that they won a clear victory, but it turned out to be costly. As a result of this shocking defeat, Britain immediately adopted a much more aggressive approach to the war, rushing seven regiments of reinforcements to Natal, and as a result the Zulus were soon overwhelmed.

What was 'Greek Fire'?

Greek Fire was the name given to a sensationally destructive incendiary weapon devised by the Byzantine Empire in the 7th century AD, which seems to have been a kind of early version of napalm. The exact composition of Greek Fire was such a highly prized secret that within a few centuries it seems to have been completely lost, even to the Byzantines themselves. Even to this day, no one is quite sure how Greek Fire was made, although there are a number of compelling theories.

The invention of Greek Fire came at a key time for the Byzantine Empire, which was being overrun by the Muslim conquests. Syria, Palestine and Egypt had all been lost to the Arab Caliphate, leaving the imperial capital of Constantinople vulnerable. In around 672 AD, the Muslims began the first of two major sieges of the city, but were repelled both times, largely thanks to Greek Fire. Greek Fire was a terrifying and vicious weapon, which could destroy entire ships, and burn the flesh from its victims. Many soldiers would desert their posts and flee rather than face the flames.

Although we may not know quite how Greek Fire was produced, there are enough contemporary descriptions of it to clearly describe how it worked. Greek Fire seems to have been most effective as a naval flamethrower, which shot a stream of burning tar from large, pressurised siphons on board the Byzantine ships, which would somehow light the mixture as it was fired towards the enemy's ships. Greek Fire could be projected up to around 50 feet, and as it was discharged it made a great thunderous noise, as it seemed to gush out of the siphons' bronze mountings, which were designed to look like a lion's mouth or some other intimidating creature. Greek Fire would burn on the surface of water, and some accounts stated that it was even ignited by water. Consequently, it was very difficult to extinguish.

Based on these descriptions, historians have come up with a range of theories for how Greek Fire was made and discharged. Some argue that its main ingredient was salt-petre, the basis of early gunpowder, which would explain the noise and smoke as it was fired. Others feel that quick-lime must have been involved, as quicklime is ignited by water. However, quicklime would not have much effect in the open sea, and there are no other accounts of saltpe-tre being used in European warfare until the 13th century. Consequently, the most likely explanation seems to be that Greek Fire was composed of a mixture of crude oil, or 'naptha', and plant resin, or 'pitch', to make the mixture thick and sticky.

Although Greek Fire was particularly effective in naval battles, it was also used on land. Flamethrowers were mounted along the exterior walls of the city of Constantinople, to drive off any invaders. The Byzantines even devised a handheld version of the flamethrower, which could be used to defend the city walls against siege towers. Thanks in large part to the incredible effectiveness of Greek Fire, Constantinople man-aged to hold off the Muslim invaders for seven hundred years, until the city finally fell to the Ottoman Turks in 1453.

Why is the wireless phone service called Bluetooth?
This might not sound like something that belongs in a

book about history, but bear with me. Bluetooth is a system for transmitting data wirelessly between electronic devices, particularly mobile phones and computers. It was designed by the Swedish company Ericsson, in partnership with a number of other leading technology companies, and the idea was to create an open technological standard that could be used by all sorts of devices, even if they were made by different companies, and ran different operating systems. Bluetooth works by transmitting a radio signal over a very short range, and on a frequency which is otherwise unused. Bluetooth can work anywhere in the world, and it send data 20 times faster than standard phone lines. It can even transmit data around corners, making it superior to similar infrared technology.

But why does it have such a strange name? The answer is that the system was named after a Danish king called Harald Bluetooth, who ruled from 940-985 AD. Harald Bluetooth is regarded as being one of the more enlightened leaders of the age, who was responsible for converting Denmark to Christianity. King Harald also united the various provinces of Denmark, which had previously tended to be at almost constant war with one another. He also took control of Norway and Sweden, uniting much of Scandinavia. Thus, Bluetooth technology was named after King Harald because he managed to foster communication between disparate groups, speaking different languages, where there had been no communication before, just as Bluetooth itself aims to connect devices which would otherwise be unable to communicate with one another. The Bluetooth logo reflects this, as it is a combination of the old runic letters 'H' and 'B', which stand for Harald Bluetooth's initials:

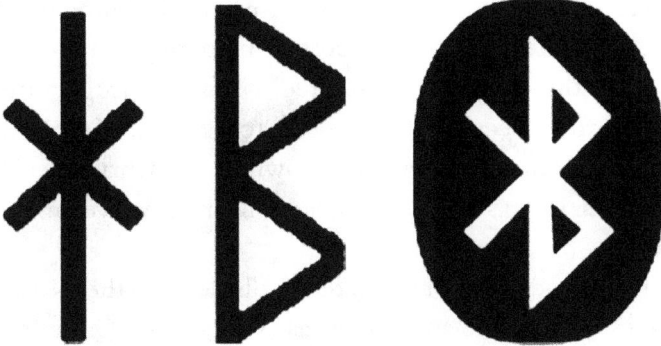

The runic letters 'H' and 'B'   Bluetooth logo

So we now know why the wireless system is called Bluetooth, but why was Harald himself known as 'Bluetooth'? This question takes us back more than a thousand years, and is therefore more of a challenge, as the sources suggest a number of possible explanations. One story holds that King Harald loved to eat blueberries, and these would stain his teeth blue, but this sounds pretty implausible. Another theory is that he had a dead tooth, which is perfectly possible, although dead teeth tend to turn grey or brown rather than blue. The most likely explanation therefore is that Bluetooth is a mistranslation of the old Danish 'Blåtand', meaning dark-skinned ('blå') great man ('tan').

Why was William I known as 'William the Conqueror'?
As every English schoolboy used to learn, in 1066 England was invaded by William the Conqueror, who defeated King Harold II at the Battle of Hastings. Harold had been hindered by having to endure a four-day forced march to the North, before fighting two battles against a Viking army led by Harald Hardråda, and then having to immediately march his victorious army south to Hastings. After victory against

Harold's understandably weary forces, William quickly secured southern England, before marching on London. There the throne was surrendered to him by Edgar Ætheling, who had been hastily chosen to succeed Harold, but who had probably not yet been crowned. On Christmas Day, 1066, William was crowned King William I at Westminster Abbey.

This period is of course traditionally deemed the 'Norman Conquest', with William known as 'William the Conqueror', but the implication that William was a foreign invader with no rightful claim to the throne is incorrect. In fact, William arguably had a better claim to the English throne than any of the other contenders, including King Harold himself. At the end of 1065, King Edward the Confessor had fallen into a coma, without clearly choosing a successor, although he may have asked that his widow and the kingdom be put under the 'protection' of Harold, who was at this time known as Harold Godwinson. When Edward died in January 1066, he left no direct heirs, and so there were a number of claimants for the succession.

Harold was Edward's brother-in-law, and he had also won the crucial support of the Witenagemot, the council of Anglo-Saxon nobles which traditionally decided the succession. However, William II, Duke of Normandy was also related to Edward, as his great aunt Emma was Edward's mother. Furthermore, Edward was believed to have verbally promised William the throne, when he visited London in 1052. Edward also had a great-nephew, the aforementioned Edgar Ætheling, who might be considered to have had a better claim than either of them, but at just 14 years of age he had no support among the nobility, as he was considered to be too young to rule. Finally, there was the Norwegian king Harald Hardråda, whose claim was the most tenuous, as it was based on an agreement made between Viking rulers during the 1040s.

In determining who was the rightful king, perhaps the key issue concerns Harold's trip to Normandy in 1064, during which he became shipwrecked. Harold became the prisoner of the Count of Ponthieu, but William rescued him, and the two of them then fought together against Brittany. William knighted Harold, and Harold swore loyalty to William, a promise which included supporting William's claim to the English throne. Harold later claimed that, being in William's possession at the time, he had no choice but to submit to an oath which was not binding, because it had been given under duress, and because it concerned a kingship which Harold did not yet have the right to confer on anyone. William, on the other hand, argued that Harold's oath meant that he could not accept the crown without perjuring himself, and thus automatically rendering his kingship illegitimate.

What was the 'Wind Trade'?

This was the name given to the world's first speculative financial bubble, which took place in 1636-7 in the United Provinces, now known as the Netherlands. The bubble was also known as Tulipomania, as it concerned the market for tulips, flowers which had only recently been introduced to the country, and which were both extremely beautiful and extremely rare. The bubble was known as the 'Wind Trade' because, although people were paying huge fortunes for the option of owning future tulip bulbs, hardly any bulbs physically changed hands, so the trade was seen to be as ephemeral and insubstantial as the wind.

Although the tulip is now closely associated with Holland, it was only introduced to that country in the late 16th century, having been cultivated for centuries in Turkey and western and central Asia. The tulip's arrival in the United Provinces coincided with a boom in wealth among the Dutch merchant class, who were becoming rich through the lucrative East Indies trade, and were keen to find exotic ways to show off their newfound affluence .

Tulips were ideal for the purpose, for a number of reasons. Firstly, they were extraordinarily beautiful. According to contemporary sources, tulips had were quite breathtaking when they were first seen in Europe, as their colours were so much brighter and more intense than native blooms. Tulips were also fascinating because of their sheer variety. Many types of tulip would produce flowers of a single colour, but the most highly prized strains produced rims, flares and veins of different, contrasting colours, creating dramatic combinations. The most celebrated of all was the Semper Augustus, a tulip which was said to combine an astounding palette of intense reds, blues, and whites.

The beauty of tulips was heightened by their rarity, particularly in the case of the more exotic varieties. In 1624, there were believed to be only 12 Semper Augustus bulbs in the whole of the United Provinces, and they were all owned by a single individual. Furthermore, the rarity of tulips was something that was unlikely to change, because the cultivation of tulips is an incredibly slow process, and there is no easy way to quickly increase the numbers. Tulips can be grown from seed, but the process takes between 7 and 12 years. There is a quicker method to cultivate new bulbs from the buds of flowering tulips, but even this method will only produce one or two bulbs per year, and the parent bulb is soon depleted.

Tulips only bloom for around a week, in April and May, and bulbs can only be uprooted and moved between June and September. As a result, tulips had what economists call 'scarcity power'.

Everyone wanted tulips, but there weren't many to buy, and so prices soared. As people noticed this rise in prices, tulips also became seen as an attractive investment, and so even more people wanted to buy them. Exchanges were set up in taverns all over the country, with bulbs notionally changing hands a dozen times in a single day, all while lying underground in someone's plot of earth. In the winter of 1636-7, the tulip frenzy reached its peak. People were said to be selling everything they owned just to get involved in the tulip market, with single bulbs reaching astonishing prices. In Hoorn, an entire house was traded for just three tulip bulbs. One merchant traded a package of goods worth 2,500 florins for a single bulb of the Viceroy tulip – at the time, a skilled worker would earn around 150 florins per year. Another offered 12 acres of land for a single bulb of Semper Augustus. At the peak of the trade, one rare Violetten Admirael van Enkhuizen bulb was sold for 5,200 florins.

The market crash seems to have taken place on February 5 1637. One of the richest men in Alkmaar, a merchant named Wouter Bartelmiesz Winkel, had died. On February 5, his estate was auctioned by his seven orphaned children, and this estate included 75 of the rarest, most valuable tulip specimens, as well as many other, less valuable varieties. This sudden flooding of the market may have tipped the balance of supply and demand, as soon flower exchanges were finding there were no bidders, only sellers, and rumours quickly spread that the market was crashing. Within days, a tulip which had previously sold for 5,000 florins was now worth only 50, with most being worth only 1 percent of their previous value.

Tulip Mania is often cited in reference to contemporary speculative episodes, such as the dotcom bubble of the late 1990s, or the more recent housing bubble, but the tulip bubble seems to have been different in a number of significant ways. Tulips were not traded on any official Dutch stock exchange, and this seems to be one reason why the crash had little effect on the wider Dutch stock market. Furthermore, although the price of tulips crashed, this does not seem to have caused the kind of economic misery that might be expected, for two reasons. Firstly, the trading seems to have taken place largely among a small group of extremely wealthy merchants, who were consequently somewhat cushioned from their losses. Secondly, and more importantly, it seems that most of the contracted tulip sales never actually took place, as the market crashed before the bulbs, and therefore also the cash, could change hands. In response to the crash, the Dutch government made a legal ruling that traders could buy their way out of their contracts by paying only a penalty of just 3.5 percent of the agreed sale price, and so as a result these trades effectively became what are known in financial terms as 'option trades', which comparatively carry a much smaller level of risk.

One of the most extraordinary things about the story of the Wind Trade was the cause of the strange and beautiful multi-coloured varieties of tulips that appeared. Normally, tulips in the wild only grow flowers of a single colour, usually red, yellow or white. It turns out that the source of the intensity and variety of the Dutch tulip colours was actually a type of mosaic virus, known as the 'Tulip breaking virus', which was unique to the tulip. Thus, these highly prized varieties of tulip, for which people were paying a small fortune, were not even distinct varieties at all, they were simply diseased flowers.

What was a 'coffin ship'?

'Coffin ship' was a term which emerged with the boom in merchant shipping during the 19ᵗʰ century. Seafaring had always been a perilous occupation, but a new source of danger emerged with the rise in international trade, as ships were now frequently overinsured, which meant that they were worth more to their owners sunk than afloat. Conditions on board were subject to barely any regulations, and as a result crews were often exposed to appalling risks. Shipowners would send out vessels which were so tatty and rotten that they would fall apart while at sea, drowning those on board. Such ships, which came to be known as 'coffin ships', would feature decayed beams, rotten joints, and 'devil bolts', which were fake bolts, designed to give the appearance of safety, but which didn't actually hold anything together. Shipowners would also often overload their ships with cargo, hire incompetent crewmen, or send unsuitable small vessels on dangerous transocean voyages, any of which could lead to a healthy insurance payout if the boat sank.

The term became particularly associated with the migration of Irish people to America, in the wake of the devastating Great Irish Famine. In one case, a ship sailed out of port at Liverpool, and then sank within sight of land, in full view of the families and well wishers who had just waved off their loved ones. If the ships did manage to make it out of port, conditions on board were so bad that mortality rates of 30 percent and upwards were not unusual, and there were stories of sharks following the ships, lured by the steady stream of dead bodies that were thrown overboard. Unscrupulous shipowners would provide their passengers with as little food, water, and living space as they could get away with, and as result dysentery, cholera, and typhus were rife.

Furthermore, many of those on board had been forced to emigrate, or deceived about the conditions they would face. As the Famine took hold, around 500,000 Irish were evicted from their homes, either through the court system, or often simply by landlords paying tenants to take their families and emigrate. These landlords would routinely promise tenants money, food, and clothing, claiming that they would be paid between two and five pounds by agents in British North America on arrival, depending on the size of the family in question. Many took up the offer of a new life, but once they arrived in Canada, no agents were ever found.

Even if the emigrants did survive the journey across the Atlantic, many of them would die while waiting to make land, as quarantine facilities became overloaded. At the Grosse Isle quarantine station outside Quebec, the summer of 1847 saw 40 ships waiting in a line more than two miles long down the St. Lawrence river, with more than 3,000 emigrants dying on the island in that year alone.

Conditions began to improve from the 1870s onwards, thanks largely to the efforts of the campaigning British MP Samuel Plimsoll. Plimsoll introduced the 'load line', a line which was to be painted on each ship to marked the highest point at which cargo could be stored, to prevent ships from being overladen. This measure was later replaced by a calculation of 'reserve buoyancy', which is the proportion of the ship's capacity above the water in relation to the capacity of the part immersed. However, the regulations introduced during Plimsoll's lifetime only went so far as requiring ships to have a load line, without legally establishing where the line should be set. As a result, many shipowners continued to display their contempt for any kind of maritime regulations, with one skipper from Cardiff expressing his opinion of the new

load line rules by painting the line on the funnel of his steam-
ship.

What was the 'Loose Box'?

This was the crude nickname given to the seating area set
aside at King Edward VII's coronation for his many mistresses. Edward was a notorious adulterer, whose infidelities
seem to have been tolerated by his wife, Queen Alexandra.
Edward was linked to more than fifty women during his marriage, and his long-term mistresses included the actress Lillie
Langtry, who built a successful stage career out of her noto-
riety; and Alice Keppel, whose great-granddaughter Camilla
Parker-Bowles would, in a strange parallel, become mistress
to Edward's great-great grandson, Prince Charles, before
becoming his official consort after their marriage in 2005. In
1869, MP Sir Charles Mordaunt threatened to name Edward
as co-respondent in his divorce case, and although this indignity was eventually avoided, Edward was called as a witness in
the case, which nonetheless caused considerable scandal. He
was also involved in another public furore over illegal gambling, which again saw him appear as a witness in court.

Edward was generally regarded as something of a playboy
and libertine, in contrast to his upright parents Victoria and
Albert, and perhaps in reaction to the strict upbringing they
had imposed upon him. From the age of seven, Edward had
undergone a strict programme of education devised by Prince
Albert, before being sent to the universities of Edinburgh,
Oxford, and Cambridge. The one thing Edward really wanted
do was serve in the army, but this was out of the question
because he was heir to the throne. Edward was not a natural
student, and his mother Victoria seems to have generally disapproved of him, finding him vain and boring. She wrote to

her daughter, Princess Victoria, 'Poor Bertie! He vexes us so much. There is not a particle of reflection, or even attention to anything but dress! I only hope he will meet with some severe lesson to shame him out of his ignorance and dullness.'

The relationship between Edward and his mother never recovered after Prince Albert's death, which Victoria quite unreasonably blamed on Edward. In 1861, Edward had been allowed to attend military manoeuvres in Ireland, and during his stay his fellow cadets had decided to smuggle an actress by the name of Nellie Clifton into his tent. When Prince Albert heard about this he was outraged, and travelled to Ireland to admonish his son. At some point on the trip, Albert fell ill with typhoid fever, and he died within two weeks. Victoria was inconsolable, and blamed Edward for her beloved Albert's death, claiming she could never forgive him. She wrote to her daughter Princess Victoria, 'I never can, or shall, look at him without a shudder.'

In hindsight, Victoria's disappointment in her son seems particularly sad, not just because it was deeply unfair, but also because Edward does seem to have been much more moral and responsible than his mother was able to give him credit for. On a tour of India, he was offended by the racist way that the British officers treated the natives, and wrote home: 'Because a man has a back face and a different religion from our own, there is no reason why he should be treated as a brute.' He insisted that the 'n' word was offensive and unacceptable, at a time when it was routinely used. He also openly counted many Jewish people among his friends, at a time when anti-Semitism was rife. Apart from his infidelities, he seems to have been a loving husband and father, who enjoyed a far closer relationship with his children than two centuries of his Hanoverian predecessors had managed.

After Albert's death, Victoria withdrew almost completely from public life, and Edward was often sent to represent her at state occasions, although he was not trusted to take part in politics or affairs of state. When he eventually succeeded to the throne after his mother's death in 1901, he had been heir apparent for more than 59 years, longer than anyone else in history, although by the time you read this he will most likely have been overtaken by Prince Charles, in another strange parallel, as Charles has been heir apparent since 1952. If Queen Elizabeth II remains on the throne until 21 April 2011, Charles will become the longest serving heir apparent.

Despite his dissolute reputation, over the course of his relatively short reign Edward became one of Britain's most popular kings, who was widely praised for his charm and diplomacy. He restored some of the splendour and spectacle to the monarchy, which had been considerably diminished during the gloomy, austere reign of Victoria, and he played a useful role in foreign policy, aided by the fact that he was related to almost every head of state in Europe – he was consequently nicknamed the 'Uncle of Europe'.

However, one relative to whom he never warmed was his nephew, Kaiser Wilhelm II of Germany, as Edward suspected Wilhelm would pursue war in Europe. Four years after the Edward's death in 1910, he was proved to have been correct, as Europe descended into the Great War.

Why are the British royal family called 'Windsor'?
Since the reign of George V, the British royal family have been known as the House of Windsor, but the origins of this name tell an interesting and revealing story about the flexible nature of royal protocol. When George V acceded to the throne in 1910, after the death of his father Edward VII, he

did so as a member of the House of Saxe-Coburg and Gotha, the dynasty of his grandfather Prince Albert. The origins of this house were of course German, and in fact the British royal family had been chiefly German in descent for a long time, since George I took to the throne in 1714, as the first British monarch of the House of Hanover.

However, the First World War polarised the question of the King's fundamental loyalty as never before, particularly as one of Germany's heavy aircraft which had begun bombing London was the unhelpfully named Gotha G.IV. Unlike some of his predecessors, George was born in England, spoke English as his first language, and considered himself to be English, and so he resented the implication that his loyalties were divided. He was said to be furious when he heard that Prime Minister David Lloyd George had said, 'I wonder what my little German friend has got to say to me,' on one of his trips to Buckingham Palace.

George's first cousin Nicholas II, the Tsar of Russia, was forced to abdicate on 15 March 1917, and suddenly all of Europe's monarchies seemed under threat. It was therefore imperative that George clarify his allegiance, and so on 17 July 1917, George issued a Royal Proclamation, declaring that henceforth he and his descendants would be known as the House of Windsor, and use the surname 'Windsor'. German relatives were stripped of their British titles and honours, and other branches of the royal family also had their names anglicised, so that Battenbergs for example became Mountbattens, in a rough translation of the German.

So why did George choose the name 'Windsor'? The answer is simply that it sounded appropriately British - or rather, English - with the right whiff of tradition and heritage, aided by the connection to the royal family's Windsor Castle.

Other names were also considered, including Plantagenet, York, Lancaster, Tudor-Stuart and, rather bluntly, England. One other name under consideration was FitzRoy, which would have been a strange choice, given that the prefix 'Fitz' was usually understood to denote illegitimacy.

So does this mean that the royal family today are all called Windsor? In fact, it doesn't, because the issue has since been complicated by Queen Elizabeth's marriage to Prince Philip, whose surname is Mountbatten (as Philip is a descendant of the aforementioned Battenbergs). The royal family have stated that all of Elizabeth's direct descendants should take the surname Mountbatten-Windsor, except for those carrying the title of prince or princess, whose surname is simply Windsor.

In practice, however, these rules don't seem to be strictly observed, and a range of surnames have been used. Some of Elizabeth's children have used the surname Mountbatten-Windsor rather than Windsor; for example, Princess Anne used it in the marriage register at Westminster Abbey when marrying Captain Mark Phillips in 1973. Many of them also use their title as a surname, so Princes Charles, William and Harry have all used 'Wales' as a last name – Harry and William were known as 'Wales' at Eton, for example. Prince Edward, Earl of Wessex, has gone by Edward Windsor professionally, and sometimes Edward Wessex, while his wife styles herself Sophie Wessex.

In truth, the reason the protocol is rather hazy when it comes to royal surnames is simply that they very rarely need one. Even after her divorce from Prince Charles, Diana never went back to her maiden name of Spencer. Instead, she simply went by 'Diana', which served perfectly well.

6

THE BODY POLITIC

'The past is a foreign country;
they do things differently there.'
L. P. Hartley (1895-1972)

What was unusual about the trial of Pope Formosus?

The man who would become Pope Formosus was born
in around 816, although his birth name has been lost
to history. He rose through the church, becoming Cardinal
Bishop of Porto, a town just south of Rome, in 864. In 872
he was a candidate for the papacy itself, but after losing out to
Pope John VIII, he found himself under attack from the new
pontiff. Pope John convened a synod (which means a church
meeting or council) to hear various charges against Formosus,
including that he had conspired against the Holy See, deserted
his diocese without papal permission, and despoiled the clois-
ters in Rome. Under threat of excommunication, Formosus
was banished from Rome.

In 883 Pope John was succeeded by Pope Marinus I, and
Formosus returned to favour, and to his diocese of Porto. Two

further popes followed Marinus, before Formosus himself was elected in 891. Formosus is considered to have been a spiritual man, and a good pope in the context of the times, but he soon made a number of important enemies, including the powerful Spoleto family. Despite this, Formosus held on to his position until his death in 896, when he was succeeded by Pope Boniface VI. Boniface's reign lasted for just 15 days, after which he was probably forced out by the Spoleto camp, who handed the papacy to Pope Stephen VI, one of Formosus's former enemies.

Stephen now decided to put the deceased Formosus on trial, in what has become known as the Cadaver Synod. Formosus's body was dug up, dressed in papal robes, and seated on a throne. The prosecution was led by Pope Stephen himself, who ranted furiously at the corpse, charging Formosus with the same offences he had faced under Pope John VIII. A young deacon was appointed to speak on Formosus's behalf, but he wisely said little. Technically, Formosus had been guilty of some of the charges. He had broken the canon prohibiting the transfer of bishops from one See to another, and he was also guilty of coveting the papacy, but no one thought it wise to point out to Pope Stephen that he himself was equally guilty of the same offences.

The verdict was a formality, and Formosus was declared to have been unworthy of the pontificate, and so all his actions were annulled, which meant that any bishops consecrated by him, and indeed any priests ordained by them, were no longer valid, which caused enormous confusion. The papal vestments were ripped from Formosus's corpse, and the three fingers used to give papal blessings were cut from his right hand. Formosus's body was then thrown into the Tiber, but it was later retrieved by a monk.

After this, things became even more absurd. When Stephen died in 897, Formosus's body was laid to rest in St Peter's, before being exhumed and put on trial a second time, by Pope Sergius III in 904. This time, the body was beheaded, and Sergius insisted that any cleric ordained by Formosus, or ordained by any cleric who in turn had been ordained by Formosus, must be re-ordained. This proved far too confusing, and so after Sergius's death, the church simply ignored his decree. Sergius's papacy was the first of a sordid and bloody sixty-year period which has come to be known as the 'Pornocracy', meaning the 'Rule of the Harlots', as the papacy was controlled by the women of the Tusculum family, led by the matriach Theodora, who was described by the 10th century historian Liutprand of Cremona as a 'shameless whore'.

What unusual present did Roger Mortimer send home to his wife Maud in 1265?

The answer is: the severed head of Simon de Montfort, as well as certain other, unspecified parts of his anatomy. These gory relics were Roger's prize for having taken a key role in defeating de Montfort's forces, and having personally killed de Montfort himself. We might imagine that Maud would have been somewhat horrified by this gruesome gift, but in fact she seems to have been made of sterner stuff. Maud was actively involved in the conflict, and it was she who had arranged the escape of Prince Edward, who led the victorious royalist forces. Far from being horrified, Maud laid on a great banquet at Wigmore Castle in celebration of her husband's victory, with de Montfort's head on prominent display, still stuck on the point of Mortimer's lance.

De Montfort's death had taken place at the Battle of Evesham, which effectively marked the end of the Second

Barons' War, which was a civil war between the Royalist supporters of England's King Henry III, and the barons, led by Simon de Montfort. The war was the result of considerable dissatisfaction with Henry's extravagance, greed, and favouritism towards certain foreign relations, while England was undergoing a widespread famine.

The Second Baron's War broke out in 1264, after Henry refused to accept the barons' long-held demands for him to give more power to the baronial council. Despite being heavily outnumbered, de Montfort successfully defeated Henry at the Battle of Lewes, making de Montfort the effective ruler of England. However, a year later he became cut off from the main body of his forces, and was slaughtered by royalist Roger Mortimer at Evesham. De Montfort's body was cut up, with various parts being given as prizes to those nobles who had played a key role in his defeat.

However, although Simon de Montfort's rule was very brief, lasting just 1 year and 82 days from 1264-5, it is regarded as one of the most significant periods in the history of democracy, because it marked the very first elected parliament in medieval Europe. Rather than simply replacing the king himself, de Montfort established a parliament, and called on each borough to send two elected representatives. It was therefore an early model of the House of Commons, and a key precursor of the modern version of democratic, representative parliament. De Montfort's legacy was hugely important, because even after he was killed, and Henry was reinstated, parliaments continued to be summoned.

Which queen was unusually devoted to her husband?

Juana of Castile is today better known as Juana the Mad, such has been history's rather unkind assessment. She was born in

Toledo in 1479, to Isabella I of Castile and Ferdinand II of Aragon, who were the first monarchs to unite the kingdoms of Spain. Juana was the third child, and so she was an *infanta*, not expected to inherit her parents' thrones, but this changed after the deaths of her older siblings. Juana was an intelligent and accomplished young lady, who excelled in dance, music and equestrianism, and spoke six languages.

Juana's education had been developed specifically to prepare her for a political marriage, and in 1496 she became engaged to Philip, Duke of Burgundy, who was known by the rather complimentary nickname of Philip the Handsome. Philip was the son of the Habsburg Holy Roman Emperor Maximilian I, and so the marriage would unite Juana's Spanish Trastámara family with the Habsburgs, creating a major European dynasty.

Although the marriage was intended as a political union, Juana and Philip fell passionately in love. In nine years, they had six children, who would between them rule much of Europe, as the two boys would each become Holy Roman Emperor, and the four girls would become queens of France, Portugal, Denmark, and Bohemia. However, although the marriage was passionate, it was not a happy union, as Juana was extremely jealous, and Philip was frequently unfaithful. Juana's obsessive resentment of Philip's mistresses may have been the first sign of her mental instability. On one occasion, she attacked one of Philip's suspected mistresses with a pair of scissors, and hacked off her hair. As she became increasingly temperamental and unstable, Philip would refuse to see her for days on end. Juana would remain locked away in her bedroom, crying herself to sleep, or furiously bashing herself against the walls.

Juana's mother Isabella I died in 1504, which meant that she now became the Queen of Castile, and her father Ferdinand II lost his title of King of Castile, as this was only held *de jure uxoris*, meaning 'by the right of his wife'. This led to the first of a series of unpleasant power struggles which would blight Juana's life, and probably cause her descent into madness. Ferdinand refused to accept that he was no longer king, and continued to issue coins in his name, and threatened to go to war with Philip, whom he hated. Philip himself was keen to reign in Castile, and so the two men came to an agreement to exclude Juana from any power, claiming that she was too mentally unstable to rule. Juana never agreed to any of this, but the decision was taken out her hands by the parliament of Castile, the *Cortes*, and she was sidelined. Soon after this agreement, Philip died, possibly of typhoid, or perhaps more likely by poisoning, courtesy of Ferdinand.

If Juana had not been mad before, the death of her husband seems to have tipped her over the edge. As his funeral cortege travelled on the long journey to Granada, she followed it devotedly, and was said to have regularly had the coffin opened so that she could kiss her dead husband's feet. Apparently, observers did not find this display of devotion particularly shocking at first, but after several months, the body was in an advanced state of decay, and yet Juana insisted on continuing the grisly ritual.

After Philip's death, control of Castile and Aragon was held in Juana's name, but without her consent, by her father Ferdinand II, her son Carlos I, and her grandson, who was confusingly known as Ferdinand I of Spain. From 1509 onwards Juana was kept imprisoned in the Santa Clara convent in Tordesillas, near Valladolid, in a windowless cell. By this point she certainly was mad, fearing that the nuns were trying to kill her, and refusing to eat, sleep, wash, or change her clothes. Today, it is generally thought that she suffered from bipolar disorder or schizophrenia. However, it is likely that Juana's madness was largely caused by her confinement, and the treatment she received from her own family. In 1555 Juana died, at the age of 75, having been imprisoned for almost 40 years. She was buried next to her husband in the Royal Chapel of Granada.

What unusual object did Lady Raleigh keep in her handbag?

The answer is the head of her late husband, the great English sailor and adventurer Sir Walter Raleigh. Raleigh was one of the leading explorers of the Elizabethan age, who founded the unsuccessful Roanoke Island colony in Virginia in 1585, and played a key role in popularising tobacco in Europe. On one occasion, one of Raleigh's servants threw a bucket of water over him, not realising that his master's pipe was supposed to be smoking, thinking that this was an indication that Raleigh was on fire. Raleigh is also popularly thought to have been the first European to bring back potatoes from the New World, but in fact the Spanish had got there first, and potatoes had been seen in England at least as early as 1569.

Elizabeth Throckmorton was one of Queen Elizabeth's ladies-in-waiting, and is said to have been a spirited and intelligent woman. She began a relationship with Sir Walter Raleigh, and fell pregnant in the summer of 1591. It was clearly a love match, as the pair quickly married in secret, and Elizabeth gave birth to a boy, whom the couple named Damerei. However, Queen Elizabeth required her ladies-in-waiting to ask her permission before marrying, and so when she found out about the marriage, she had Raleigh imprisoned in the Tower of London, and banished his new wife from court. Despite this, the couple remained committed to one another, although Raleigh was out of favour at court for a number of years. The dashing, handsome Raleigh had previously been one of the queen's favourites, which may explain her lengthy and bitter retribution.

Raleigh eventually regained the Queen's favour, but after her death in 1603, his position because precarious. Not only was Raleigh an embarrassing throwback to a past, anti-Spanish age, he had also been openly hostile to Catholicism, which automatically made him the focus of suspicion under the new Catholic king James I. Raleigh was arrested and imprisoned soon after Elizabeth's death, and charged with treason, for his alleged involvement in a conspiracy against King James known as the 'Main Plot', on the flimsiest of evidence. Raleigh conducted his own defence, but was convicted and sent to the Tower, where he remained for thirteen years.

In 1616, he was released, so that he could sail to South America to search for the legendary city of gold, 'El Dorado'. However, by this time King James had made peace with Spain, and so when a group of Raleigh's men attacked a Spanish outpost at San Tomé, off the coast of Guyana, the furious Spanish ambassador demanded Raleigh's execution, despite the fact that the attack had been carried out in direct contravention of Raleigh's explicit orders. King James however was keen to appease the Spanish, and so on 29 October 1618, Raleigh was beheaded at Whitehall. As he waited for the axe to fall, his final words were, 'Strike, man, strike!'.

After Raleigh's execution, his body was buried in St Margaret's Church, next to Westminster Abbey. His head, however, was embalmed and presented to Lady Raleigh, who then carried it around with her in a red bag for the rest of her life, a further 29 years. When meeting guests, she would ask them if they would like to see Walter, and then produce the withered relic from her handbag. After he death, this grotesque heirloom was passed on to her son, Carew, but when he died it was finally buried with him.

Who was the worst executioner in history?

One of the strangest episodes of 17th century England was the Popish Plot, an absurd, unfounded witchhunt in which many leading figures were falsely accused of being Catholics, and punished by execution. The climate of fear was exacerbated by the nature of the executions, as some of them were handled by Jack Ketch, who may well deserve the title of the 'worst executioner in history'. In 1683 at Tower Hill, Ketch carried out the public execution of Lord William Russell, who had been condemned as a Catholic. Russell apparently paid Ketch to make a clean job of it, and when the first blow of the axe merely glanced his neck, he looked up and complained, 'You dog! Did I give you ten guineas to use me so inhumanly?' In the end, it took Ketch four or five attempts to sever Russell's head.

After the incident, there was such a public outcry at Ketch's incompetent performance that he published a pamphlet to defend himself, denying the circulating rumours that he had been either drunk, or deliberately cruel. He explained that the poor execution was the fault of Lord Russell himself, who did not, 'dispose himself as was most suitable.' Ketch may have been incompetent, but his executions soon drew larger crowds than anyone else's, as the public clamoured for the drama of a Jack Ketch performance, in which the victims would understandably quiver with fear. He became so notorious that the name 'Jack Ketch' became used as a generic term for any hangman, executioner, and sometimes even for death itself.

Two years later, Ketch was once again called in action, for the execution of James Scott, the Duke of Monmouth. Scott was aware of the fiasco of Lord Russell's execution, and urged Ketch not to repeat it, paying him six guineas upfront, and promising six more for a clean kill. He even inspected Ketch's axe, and demanded to know if it was sharp enough. However, all of this seems to have only served to make Ketch even more nervous, and after Scott knelt on the scaffold, Ketch hacked away so ineptly that even after six blows, Scott was still not dead, but writhing and screaming in agony. As the crowd roared with horror, Ketch threw down his axe, and sulkily refused to continue, challenging anyone in the crowd to take over if they thought they could do better. As the victim knelt bleeding on the block, the sheriff ordered Ketch to pick up the axe and finish the job. He eventually did so, after two further attempts, but even then he had failed to sever the head, and had to complete the task with a butcher's knife, soaking the scaffold and nearby spectators with blood. According to reports, the crowd were so horrified and enraged that Ketch had to be escorted away for his own safety.

The explanation for Jack Ketch's ineptitude is fairly simple. Execution, which meant beheading, was only performed on the nobility, as it was seen as an honourable form of death, whereas the common masses would simply be hanged. Because executions were generally rare, there were no professional executioners; instead, the job was given to the public hangman, even though he would often have no experience of performing an execution. Thus, when Jack Ketch carried out these beheadings, he basically had no idea what he was doing. Furthermore, a person's neck is comprised of thick muscles and vertebrae, which means it takes considerable strength and skill to sever it with one blow.

Given that this was the case, some of the blame for the botched executions must fall on King Charles II himself, for allowing them to be carried out by an untrained incompetent. By contrast, when Henry VIII had Anne Boleyn executed at Tower Hill in 1536, he still retained some affection for her, so he made a special point of hiring a skilled swordsman from France, who severed Anne's head with one clean swoop.

After the disaster of the Duke of Monmouth's execution, Jack Ketch was sacked, and imprisoned at Bridewell. His replacement was a butcher named Paskah Rose, but within four months Rose was caught stealing a coat, and hanged at Tyburn. Amazingly, despite everything that had passed, Ketch was now rehired in his place.

What happened to the heart of the Lost Dauphin?

One of the most enduring mysteries in France's history concerns the fate of the so-called 'Lost Dauphin', Louis XVII, whose parents King Louis XVI and Queen Marie Antoinette were publicly executed by guillotine in 1793, in what was the defining moment of the French Revolution. At this point their son Louis Charles, the Dauphin, effectively became the rightful king, at least in the eyes of royalists ('Dauphin' was the title given to the heir apparent to the French throne). Louis Charles was imprisoned by the Republican revolutionaries, along with his sister Marie Therese, and given the plain Republican name of Louis Charles Capet.

Louis Charles spent the next two years in prison, in conditions which were somewhere between unpleasant and barbaric, depending on which sources you consult. The reason for this disparity is that after the French monarchy was restored, accounts of the Revolutionaries tended to exaggerate their crimes, but it seems that the 8-year-old prince was almost certainly kept in solitary conditions, possibly in a windowless cell, which one way or another must have been extremely traumatic. On June 8 1795, it was announced that Louis Charles had died of tuberculosis, at the age of just 10, and the young prince was given a plain burial in an unmarked grave.

However, rumours soon began to circulate that the Dauphin had in fact escaped, having been spirited away by some sympathetic adult, and replaced by a deaf mute. These rumours were fuelled by a number of apparent irregularities. Before his death, Louis Charles had not spoken to a single person for more than six months, whereas beforehand he had been willing to speak with guards and visitors. After his death, the body had not been positively identified, even though his sister Marie Therese was still alive, and could have done so. Reports of his death described it as the culmination of a long-held malady, but previously there had been no mention of any illness. Finally, a week before Louis's death, his regular doctor died suddenly, in mysterious circumstances.

As the story of the Dauphin's substitution and escape became widely accepted, hundreds of pretenders came forward, claiming to be the Lost Dauphin, and ready to claim their inheritance. Some of them became well known, and even today some of their descendants have managed to convince small retinues of supporters. One of the most successful was a German clock-maker named Karl-Wilhelm Naundorff, who even managed to persuade Louis Charles's childhood nurse that he was the real Dauphin. The Dutch government recognised Naundorff's claim, allowing him to take the surname 'Bourbon'. When he died, his tomb was inscribed 'Louis

XVII, roi de France et de Navarre' (Louis XVII, King of France and Navarre).

Another candidate was the famous naturalist John James Audubon, who was born in the same year as Louis Charles, adopted at about the right time, and raised in France, before emigrating to America when he was 18. Audubon sent his wife an intriguing and mysterious letter when he returned to France in 1828, describing himself thus: 'patient, silent, bashful, and yet powerful of physique and of mind, dressed as a common man, I walk the streets! I bow! I ask permission to do this or that! I... who should command all!'

Another well known pretender was an American named Eleazer Williams, who was raised by a tribe of Mohawk Native Americans, before becoming a pioneer of Wisconsin, and an Episcopal minister. Williams is thought to have been the inspiration for Mark Twain's satirical figure of a conman known as the 'Lost Dauphin' in *Adventures of Huckleberry Finn*.

However, in recent years the mystery appears to have been resolved, thanks to the equally fantastical story of the Dauphin's heart. After the boy's death in 1795, his heart was cut out and stolen at his autopsy, by doctor Philippe-Jean Pelletan, who smuggled it out under his coat, and then preserved it in alcohol. In 1830, Pelletan gave the heart to the Archbishop of Paris, who then passed it on to the Austrian royal family. The heart continued on a bizarre tour of the aristocratic homes of Europe, before ending up in a crystal urn at the Basilica Saint-Denis in 1975.

In the year 2000, two separate teams of scientists in Belgium and Germany conducted DNA tests on the dessicated heart, which was by now as hard as stone, and compared it with samples of hair from Marie Antoinette and other members of her bloodline. They concluded that the heart had almost certainly belonged to a relative of Marie Antoinette, thus proving beyond any reasonable doubt that the Dauphin had in fact died in prison, which meant that all the later pretenders were bogus. The French government was convinced by these findings, and arranged for the heart to be buried in the royal crypt at the Basilica on June 8 2004, exactly 209 years after the young prince's death.

What happened to the Donner Party?

By the 1840s, the continuing westward expansion of the American settlers led to a popular belief that it was the new nation's 'manifest destiny' to expand all the way to the Pacific coast. As land in the eastern states became scarce, large groups of pioneers set off for the West, in order to establish new settlements, and claim some land of their own. They travelled in covered wagons, pulled by oxen, horses, and mules, usually in large parties known as wagon trains. The first successful wagon crossing from the East coast to the West was made in 1844, and the California Trail soon became a well established route.

In the spring of 1846, 62 year old farmer George Donner of Illinois set off with his family, as part of a huge train of more than 500 wagons. The party stuck to the well established route all the way to Fort Bridger, Wyoming, and considered their journey to have been largely uneventful. George Donner's wife Tamsen wrote in a letter: 'I never could have believed we could have travelled so far with so little difficulty. Indeed, if I do not experience something far worse than I have yet done, I shall say the trouble is all in getting started.'

Before they reached Fort Bridger, the pioneers were handed open letters which had been sent by a man named Lansford Hastings, encouraging them to take a shortcut across the Great Basin which he had discovered. Hastings had written a book, *The Emigrant's Guide to California and Oregon*, which detailed this shortcut, which he had named Hastings' Cut-Off. He explained that he had travelled this route himself to California, although never with a wagon, and that it was a smooth route, with plenty of sources of water, and without rough terrain or hostile Native Americans. By the time the Donners reached Fort Bridger, Hastings had already gone on ahead, but nonetheless they and a number of other families decided to take the shortcut. The party were further assured that Hastings would leave letters for them en route, and come back to guide them where necessary.

However, the Hastings Cut-Off proved to be completely unsuitable for wagons, and the Donner Party were soon far behind schedule. The travellers were forced to navigate treacherous canyons and steep inclines, with all the able-bodied men having to work constantly to clear the route of boulders, brush, and fallen trees, slowing their progress to just a mile and a half per day. As a result, the journey to the Great Salt Lake, which should have taken a week, took a whole month. By this point, the pioneers and their animals were exhausted, and had used up most of their food. They now had to cross the Great Salt Desert, but found that the desert was twice as big as Hastings had claimed, and the wheels of their wagons simply sank into the white salt. The party fell into disarray, losing many of their oxen into the desert, and fighting among themselves. When two of the wagons became entangled, one man was killed in the ensuing fight.

By October, the party had reached the edge of the Sierra Nevada mountains, an immense range with more than 500 peaks of over 12,000 feet in height. Thanks to its height and proximity to the Pacific coast, the mountain range receives heavy snowfall. The Donner Party had been assured that the mountains would be passable for another month, but the weather turned cold far sooner than expected, and they found themselves snowbound on the mountain pass. The heavy snow meant hunting was impossible, they had exhausted all of their supplies, and there was no grass to feed their oxen and horses.

Two makeshift camps were set up, with 60 of the group in three flimsy cabins at Truckee Lake, and 21 in tents at Alder Lake, half a day's travelling away. It was decided that a group of fifteen of the strongest men and women would forge on to try and cross the mountains, in the hope of reaching California and bringing back help. This group became known as the Forlorn Hope. With no food, and on makeshift snowshoes, their journey was exhausting and perilous. As starvation set in, the subject of cannibalism was raised. The group considered drawing lots or fighting duels, to determine who should die, so that the rest of them could eat, but decided against these ideas.

However, after five of the men died in quick succession, there seemed to be no alternative, and so their bodies were carefully cut up and labelled, before being eaten, so that none of the party would have to eat the flesh of one of their own relatives. Two Native Americans who had joined the group were then shot and eaten. Some of the settlers justified this by claiming that the pair had been close to death anyway, but this is disputed.

Conditions at the two camps left behind were equally bleak. The camps were cramped and dirty, and it was too cold to go outside. Most of those left behind were women and children. With nothing to eat, they boiled the hides and bones of their animals to make a kind of glue-like soup. Eventually the bones became so brittle that they could be chewed and eaten. The cabin roofs at Truckee Lake were made of ox-skin, and eventually one of these was removed and boiled, with the families now sharing the two remaining cabins.

The Forlorn Hope travellers eventually reached a Native American encampment, which fed them, and guided them to the nearest settlement. Once they reached California, the travellers desperately tried to arrange rescue parties, to help find their families, but all able-bodied men were required for the ongoing Mexican-American War. The first of four rescue parties eventually reached the group in mid-February 1847, around four months after they had become trapped. When they reached the two camps, the rescuers found a horrifying scene. The survivors were gaunt and withered, and barely able to move. Some had mentally disintegrated, and one woman had gone almost blind. Many of the survivors had been forced to turn to cannibalism, and there were suspicions that a number of the dead had been murdered for food.

The story of the Donner Party horrified the nation, and many of the survivors were spurned and condemned for their role in what had taken place. Of the 87 travellers who had reached the mountain range, only 48 survived. Perhaps as a result of the Donner Party tragedy, rates of migration to California quickly fell, from around 1,500 in 1846, to 450 the following year, and 400 in 1848. However, this decline was dramatically reversed in 1849, when the California Gold Rush began, and 25,000 hopefuls made their way west. Even so, the vast majority of these used the conventional California Trail, and the Hastings Cut-Off was abandoned.

How was General Custer punished for not listening?

George Armstrong Custer is one of most divisive figures in American military history. He was born in New Rumley, Ohio, and graduated bottom of his class of 34 cadets at the West Point military academy, having been threatened with expulsion in each of his four years' training. However, the outbreak of the US Civil War meant that all potential officers were needed to serve, even the dunces, and so Custer soon found himself involved in a number of prominent Union campaigns, serving with influential officers including Major General George B. McClellan, commander of the Army of the Potomac, and Major General Alfred Pleasonton, an extravagant and divisive schemer, who became Custer's mentor.

Custer was a cavalry officer, who quickly gained the respect of his men through his courageous willingness to lead the line himself, when many other officers tended to hang back from the action. Custer gained a series of promotions over the course of the Civil War, reaching the rank of 'brevet' (meaning 'temporary') Major General. As a commander, Custer's approach was marked by rapid, aggressive attacks, and he played a key role in the Appomattox Campaign, which led to the surrender of Confederate General Robert E. Lee. After the end of the Civil War, Custer drifted somewhat, and involved himself in politics rather too much for some people's tastes. He travelled West to fight in the Indian Wars against the plains-dwelling Native Americans, but rather than commanding, he was ordered to serve under General Terry, a surprising demotion which seemed to be a punishment for his political interference.

The Indian Wars were the culmination of growing tension between American settler communities and the native tribes of the Great Plains, including the Lakota Sioux and the Cheyenne. The United States repeatedly broke treaty agreements and continued to expand into the West, leading to conflict, violence, and a cycle of reprisals and distrust. The situation was exacerbated by the discovery of gold in the Black Hills of Dakota; in fact, the gold was discovered by Custer himself, while on a reconnaissance mission. Now that gold had been found, the US government was determined to take possession of this valuable territory, and so all the remaining free Plains Indians were ordered to report to reservations by January 31 1876, or else be considered hostile.

Five months later, in June 1876, Custer's scouts spotted a major camp of around 8,000 Indians along the Little Bighorn River. This enormous gathering of tribes had been summoned by a Lakota Sioux holy man named Sitting Bull, to discuss the increasingly menacing situation. Custer was expected to wait for General Terry to arrive with reinforcements, but instead he decided to attack straight away, certain that his men could defeat any Indian force, no matter how outnumbered they might be. Custer only had around 650 men under his command, and he then weakened his force further by splitting them into three battalions. Two battalions were to be led respectively by Major Marcus Reno and Captain Frederick Benteen, who would attack from the north and south of the encampment, while Custer would attack with the third battalion from the east.

As they approached the Indian encampment, Reno's men formed a skirmish line some way short of the camp, but they were quickly overrun by the Indian warriors, and retreated for the cover of trees nearby. This meant that when Custer's battalion attacked from the east, they had no support, and so they were quickly isolated, and driven up a steep ridge. Below the ridge was a five metre drop into the river, and as a result Custer and his men were effectively trapped. As the Indians closed in, Custer made his last stand, but the position was impossible, and the entire battalion were brutally massacred.

After his death, Custer became celebrated as a great American hero, and the tragic story of the Last Stand became the defining event of the Indian Wars. Custer was praised for his undeniable courage and his many victories, with his reputation being significantly burnished by a number of books written after his death by his widow Libby, who never remarried. During the Civil War, Custer had treated his Confederate opponents with courtesy and honour, and he had also been admired by the Indians for 'counting coup', seeking prestige and honour in victory, rather than annihilation. At Little Bighorn, the two battalions led by Reno and Benteen had quickly retreated, but Custer and his men stayed on the knoll and fought to the death.

On the other hand, Custer had faced significant criticism during his lifetime, and his reputation became increasingly controversial over the course of the twentieth century. While he was alive, Custer was seen by many as an attention-seeking dandy, who put his men at risk through his reckless pursuit of personal fame and glory. He was notorious for having his own uniforms specially made, making sure he stood out in shiny boots, tight olive-coloured trousers, a red cravat, and a wide-brimmed slouch hat. His career at West Point is seen by many as proof of his lack of intelligence, and although he is known to history as 'General' Custer, in fact this was only ever a temporary rank, as he was officially a lieutenant colonel. Many felt that the catastrophic defeat at Little Bighorn was indicative of Custer's recklessness and egotism, as he was determined to win a glorious victory for himself, risking his men's lives in the process. He refused to wait for reinforcements before attacking, rejected the use of Gatling guns, and then further weakened his forces by splitting them into three.

Between them, the three battalions numbered just 650 men, against a force of around 3,500 Sioux and Cheyenne warriors.

Custer is perhaps most vilified today for his role as a key figure in the appalling treatment of the Native Americans, which is perhaps the most shameful chapter in the history of the United States. However Custer himself opposed President Grant's aggressive policy towards the Indians, and jeopardised his own career by publicly criticising the many abuses carried out at the reservations.

Two days after the Battle of Little Bighorn, General Terry arrived at the ridge, to find most of the bodies had been stripped, scalped, and badly mutilated. Some of the bodies had been so thoroughly disfigured that they were unrecognisable. By contrast, Custer's body had not been badly treated, as the Cheyenne considered him one of their own, as he had been in a relationship with one of the Cheyenne women, which they considered to be a marriage. Custer's body was thus found face up, laying across the bodies of two of his men, with a strange smile on his face, which was presumably arranged after his death. There were two bullet holes, in his heart and left temple, either of which would have been fatal, which may mean that one of his men had mercifully ended his life, to prevent him being tortured. There were only two signs of Custer's body being misused. Firstly, an arrow had been jammed in his genitals. Secondly, his eardrums had been perforated by knitting needles, a punishment which the Indians later explained had been inflicted by two Cheyenne women, so that he might 'hear better in the afterlife', after having apparently forgotten his promise to Chief Rock Forehead to never again attack Native Americans.

7

SPIRITUAL STUMBLES

'Let there be no violence in religion.'
The Koran

Why was the Holy Island of Lindisfarne abandoned by its inhabitants?

Lindisfarne is one of the most magical and atmospheric places in England. It is a small, desolate tidal island off the north-east coast, which has been seen as a place of religious significance for more than a thousand years. It is a 'tidal island' because it is only an island at high tide. At low tide, you can walk to Lindisfarne from the mainland, as a causeway rises up from the sea, which adds to the island's strange, supernatural quality.

A monastery was founded on the island in the year 635, by St Aiden. Near the end of the 7th century, Saint Cuthbert was persuaded to give up his life as a hermit to become a monk at Lindisfarne, and then later became the monastery's Abbot. In the early 8th century, the monastery produced a famous manuscript known as the Lindisfarne Gospels, which was a lavish, illustrated copy of the four gospels in Latin, although some of it was also translated into Old English. The mysterious island became well established as place of pilgrimage until the 10th century, when it was abandoned by its inhabitants.

So what had happened to cause the monks to flee their spiritual home? The answer is simple: the Vikings had arrived. Thanks to its success as a site of pilgrimage, Lindisfarne's monastery had become wealthy and powerful, and this made it an ideal target for plundering. In 793, Scandinavian raiders attacked and looted the monastery, in what is believed to have been one of the very first Viking raids on the British Isles. Monks were murdered inside the abbey, thrown into the sea to drown, or carried off as slaves. The Northumbrian scholar Alcuin wrote to Ethelred, King of Northumbria, describing the horror and brutality of the attack on one of Britain's most sacred sites:

'Lo, it is nearly 350 years that we and our fathers have inhabited this most lovely land, and never before has such terror appeared in Britain as we have now suffered from a pagan race... Behold the church of St Cuthbert spattered with the blood of the priests of God, despoiled of all its ornaments; a place more venerable than all in Britain is given as a prey to pagan peoples.'

This was the beginning of the Viking Age, as coastal Britain suffered frequent and murderous attacks. The Viking raids on Lindisfarne continued for another 80 years, until the monks finally fled the island in 875, taking with them the bones of St Cuthbert, which are now buried in Durham Cathedral. Today, Lindisfarne is still a magical and lonely place, with a population of less than 200, but it is a popular site for tourists and birdwatchers.

What was the Peasants' Crusade?

Between 1096 and 1099 an enormous Christian army set out on a holy war to recapture Jerusalem, which had been conquered by the Muslim Turks in 1076. This was the triumphant First Crusade, which eventually retook the Holy City in July 1099, massacring the entire Muslim population, so that Jerusalem's streets were soon said to be ankle-deep in blood. However, just before the First Crusade there had in fact been an earlier attempt to retake Jerusalem, which became known as the Peasants' Crusade, or the People's Crusade. As the name suggests, this was a disorganised collection of peasants, women, and children, and it turned out to be a disastrous and bloody failure.

The Peasants' Crusade was inspired by the Council of Clermont in 1095, at which Pope Urban II had urged the Christian world to raise an army to retake Jerusalem, stating 'It is the will of God.' Popular support for a crusade had been spurred by a number of strange meteorological events in 1095 which were seen as positive omens, including a lunar eclipse, a meteor shower, aurora borealis, and a comet. Jerusalem was of course considered to be the holiest site in Christianity (as well as being the third holiest site of Islam, after Mecca and Medina), but while it was held by Muslims it was almost impossible for Christians to travel there safely for pilgrimage. This was the religious justification for the Crusade, but there were clearly other reasons for the conflict. The Muslim forces were posing a growing threat to the Byzantine Empire, and so there was an obvious strategic motive for the war. And the Crusaders themselves were often motivated by more prosaic goals, in particular the prospect of looting in foreign lands, and escape from the famine, drought, and plague which beset much of Europe at the time.

Preachers all over Europe took up the cause, and one of the most successful was a monk named Peter the Hermit, who gathered his army at Cologne. Peter had soon raised such a large force that, rather than waiting for the Pope's orders, he and his army decided to set off for Jerusalem immediately. This army soon gained a second leader, a veteran knight known as Walter Sans Avoir, which was French for 'Walter the Penniless', and the Crusaders now numbered somewhere between 40-80,000, although many of these were women and children, and the men who made up the bulk of the army were mostly untrained and unarmed. The army now began to march south through Europe, but their lack of military discipline and command soon became apparent, as they split into two groups, and rioted and looted in many of the cities they reached. In Belgrade, the Crusaders fought with the city's garrison, before pillaging and burning the city. In Niš, the Crusaders were soundly defeated by the city's troops, losing around a quarter of their number.

When the Crusaders did eventually reach Constantinople, the Emperor Alexius I didn't seem to know quite what to do with this chaotic rabble, although his first thought was presumably to get them out of his city. Alexius quickly sent them across the Bosphorus, despite presumably being aware that they would stand little chance against the well-armed, well-drilled forces of the Seljuk Turks. After taking the city of Xerigordon, the first party of the Crusade were soon defeated. With no water supply, the survivors were forced to drink donkey's blood and their own urine to survive. The main body of the Peasants' Crusade meanwhile marched on towards Nicaea, but they were ambushed en route, in a narrow, wooded valley where the Turkish army were waiting for them. The Crusaders were trapped, and attacked with a hail of arrows, before being massacred almost to a man. Only a few thousand made it back to Constantinople, as the only survivors of the disastrous Peasants' Crusade.

When did Christians lead a crusade against other Christians?

When we think of the Crusades today, we tend to think of them as being a conflict purely between Christians and Muslims over control of the Holy Land, but in fact there were also crusades against Jews, Slavs, Mongols, and even other Christians. The precedent was perhaps set in the Fourth Crusade, which took place between 1202 and 1204. This campaign was initially intended to recapture Jerusalem from the Seljuk Turks, but it degenerated into a conflict between the Roman Catholic church and what became later known as the Eastern Orthodox Church. There had been growing conflict between the European Crusaders and their Byzantine allies, and during the Fourth Crusade this culminated in an outright attack on Constantinople by the Crusaders, in which the city was brutally sacked and looted.

A few years later, the Catholic church launched the Albigensian Crusade, which was directed from the start at fellow Christians, and became one of the bloodiest and most destructive episodes in European history. The target of the crusade was the Cathars, who took their name from the Greek meaning 'the pure ones', who were a peaceful Christian sect found in south-west France. The Cathars believed there were two gods, rather than one. There was Rex Mundi, the evil 'king of the world', who was responsible for everything physical and corporeal, including the earth; and then there was the second god, the one that was to be worshipped, who was a purely spiritual being, the god of love and peace. As such, the Cathars attached no special significance to the Holy Land or the Holy Cross, as these were all merely physical things, things of the earth, and therefore inherently evil.

The Cathars were pacifists, who believed in the merits of healthy and constructive debate, but Pope Innocent III felt that this growing movement was too much of a threat to the authority of Rome, and so was determined to stamp it out. He first tried sending monks to convert the Cathars, but the 'pure ones' were unimpressed by the wealthy, worldly Cistercians, who lacked the piety and devotion of their leaders. Pope Innocent next sent a Spanish priest named Domingo de Guzman, who was later to become canonized as St Dominic. Domingo and his followers led a lifestyle of simple poverty, which might have been expected to impress the Cathars, but still they remained loyal to their faith.

At this point, the Pope lost patience. He announced that he would grant the Cathar's lands to any crusaders who would take up arms against them. This appealed to a great number of northern French noblemen, in particular Earl Simon de Montfort (the father of the more celebrated Simon de Montfort, who we encountered in Chapter Six), whose ruthlessness and brutality would become notorious. The war which followed lasted 20 years, from 1209-1229. The first city to fall was Béziers, whose inhabitants surrendered peacefully, but were nonetheless massacred. When the Abbot in charge was asked how he could tell the heretics from the true Catholics, he replied, 'Kill them all; God will know his own.' He wrote to Pope Innocent, boasting, 'Today your Holiness, twenty thousand heretics were put to the sword, regardless of rank, age, or sex.' As the Crusaders moved from town from town, many Cathars surrendered in the hope of mercy, but none was granted, as people across the region were cut down, or burned at the stake. In one astonishingly vicious incident, Simon de Montfort gouged out the eyes of 100 prisoners, cut off their noses and lips, and then had them led back to town by a prisoner with one remaining eye.

The Crusade was ended in 1229 by the Treaty of Paris, in which all of the Toulouse region was handed over to King Louis IX, but the persecution of the last few Cathars continued. The same year, the Catholic Church formed a Papal Inquisition, with the express purpose of pursuing the remaining Cathars. In 1244, the last remaining Cathar fortress at Montségur fell, with over 200 Cathar leaders burned in an enormous fire at the foot of the castle.

What was the Children's Crusade?

The story of the Children's Crusade is a fascinating and tragic one. There are a number of different versions, but the central elements are fairly consistent. The story goes that in 1212, following the failure of the disastrous Fourth Crusade, a young boy began preaching in France or Germany, claiming that he had been visited by Jesus, who told him to lead a crusade to take back Jerusalem by peacefully converting Muslims to Christianity.

Such was the boy's passion and conviction, he managed to raise an enormous army of children, perhaps as many as 30,000, which he then led south to the Mediterranean. There, the boy had predicted, the sea would part, allowing the Crusaders to march to the Holy Land, but when they reached the shore, disappointingly nothing happened. However, the children were unbowed, and instead managed to gain passage on a number of ships owned by merchants. Sadly, none of the children made it to the Holy Land, as one of the ships was wrecked near Sardinia in bad weather, while the children on the surviving ships were sold into slavery by the devious merchants, with many of them being forced to convert to Islam.

It's a powerful story, which has been circulated as fact for centuries, but research in the last 40 years suggests that the story of the Children's Crusade is largely apocryphal, although it does combine elements of two genuine events of 1212. Firstly, there was a popular crusade which started in Germany in that year, and then collapsed when the Mediterranean failed to part. However, the group did not board merchant ships and get sold into slavery in Africa or Arabia; instead, they mostly just went home. Some of them however may well have travelled along the coast to Marseilles, and it's there that they may have been sold into slavery.

The second genuine event was a separate movement, also in 1212, which was led by a 12 year old French boy named Stephen of Cloyes, who did indeed claim to have been visited by Jesus. He amassed a following of perhaps 30,000 people, who believed he could work miracles, but there is no evidence of any plans to go to Jerusalem. Eventually, the French king Philip II ordered the group to disband, and they seem to have obeyed.

Although both of these movements resemble the story of the Children's Crusade in some respects, there is one crucial problem, which is that neither movement was actually made up of children. This misconception seems to have arisen because of a mistranslation of the Latin word 'pueri', which could mean either 'boys' or 'young men of low status'. None of the contemporary sources describes either of these movements as being a 'children's crusade', it was only later sources which did so, presumably because of mistranslation of the Latin, or simply because a crusade made up of children makes for a much better story.

Why did the Flagellant movement fall out of favour?

Flagellants were religious ascetics who carried out an extreme form of penance by whipping themselves repeatedly. This practice of mortification of the flesh has been observed in a number of religions, and had certainly become a feature of the Catholic Church by at least the 11th century, when it was occasionally used as a form of penance as well as, more usually, punishment. One famous flagellant was Saint Dominic Loricatus, who is recorded as giving himself an astonishing (and implausible) 300,000 lashes over just six days of Lent.

At the time of Saint Dominic Loricatus, however, there was no Flagellant movement as such, it was just a rather bizarre practice carried out by a few overly zealous individuals. However, over the 13th and 14th centuries an organised movement began to appear, as a response to the horrors and hardships of the age. The first occurrence began in Perugia in 1259, as a form of penance, during a dreadful, Europe-wide famine, and an epidemic of disease. Groups of people began marching through the city, whipping themselves while singing and waving banners. The movement spread north to Austria, with reports of Jews and priests being killed by the frenzied marchers, travelling in groups of up to 10,000.

There were new Flagellant outbreaks in 1296 and 1333-4, but the movement reached its peak during the Black Death, starting in around 1347. The Black Death was one of the deadliest and most horrific plagues in human history, killing around 40-60 percent of Europe's population, with victims suffering painful black buboes in their groins, necks, and arm-pits, which dripped with blood and pus. Life was so grim and hopeless that people were willing to try anything, as the world seemed to be coming to an end. The only explanation most people could reach for was that God was punishing humanity for its litany of sins.

In this context, it is perhaps not surprising that Flagellant groups sprang up all over Europe, desperate to take the most extreme measures possible to atone for whatever sins had caused God's wrath. One group in Germany, the Brethren of the Cross, would march for thirty-three and a half days, with each day representing a year in Christ's life. Twice a day, they would perform their rituals in a public square, which involved publicly stripping off their clothes, falling violently to their knees, and gesturing with their arms in a kind of weird sema-phore to indicate their sins; adulterers would fall face down in the dirt, while perjurers would lie on their sides, raising three fingers in the air. They would then whip themselves rhythmi-cally while singing, until their flesh was bruised and bleeding. According to some reports, flagellants used whips tipped with metal studs or spikes, but it's hard to imagine how people could have survived if that was the case.

At first, the Flagellants tended to be welcomed as they arrived in each new town, in the hope that their piety and devotion would help to protect the town from plague, but over time the welcomes they received became cooler, as people began to notice that the Black Death would often appear after a visit from the Flagellants, even though it hadn't been present beforehand. Far from helping to expel the plague with their mortifications, the Flagellants were transmitting it, as they travelled from town to town. They were also becoming an increasing threat to what little social order was left, as they attacked and murdered priests, and looted churches.

By 1349, the Catholic Church was becoming increasingly worried, as the Flagellant movement was spreading rapidly, and the Flagellants were beginning to openly criticise the Church. In Germany, one group claimed they would resurrect Emperor Frederick II, who had been an outspoken enemy of the Church, and had promised to massacre the clergy. Pope Clement VI now moved against the group, condemning them in a papal bull, and ordered the clergy to suppress the movement. As the Pope's threats grew more serious, European leaders became more brutal in their treatment of Flagellants, threatening to execute any who appeared in their lands, while in Breslau one Flagellant master was burned alive. Quickly, the movement vanished.

One bizarre detail about this story is the nature of the punishments meted out to Flagellants. At one point, a Flagellant group arrived in Avignon, where the papacy was at that time based. Clement ordered the marchers to be rounded up and flogged, which seems a rather odd punishment in the circumstances.

Who was the Pope in 1409?

It sounds like a simple question, but in fact the answer is far from clear. In 1409, and until 1415, there were three people who simultaneously claimed to be pope, all holding their own rival Papal Courts. In Rome, there was Pope Gregory XII, who is now considered to have been the valid pope. In Avignon in southern France, a rival papacy had elected Benedict XIII in 1394. Meanwhile in Pisa, Italy, there was a third pope, Alexander V. So how could there be more than one pope? Surely the pope is God's sole appointed representative on earth, and by definition, therefore, there can only be one? Essentially, Catholics agreed with this principle, there was just some dispute about which pope was legitimate, while the others were deemed 'antipopes'.

The important split had taken place in 1378, after the Papal Court returned to Rome, having been based in Avignon for 69 years. (Incidentally, this period of Avignon Papacy gave rise to the name of the wine Châteauneuf-du-Pape, which means 'the pope's new castle', in reference to the papal palace in Avignon). The Roman cardinals now elected Pope Urban VI, but the French objected, and instead elected Clement VII, who took up residence in Avignon, and ruled until 1394. The issue was further complicated in 1409 by a third claimant, Alexander V, who was elected in Pisa, Italy. At this point, there were now three people claiming to be pope, all of whom had significant supporters. This particular rift was finally ended in 1417, when Pope Martin V was elected, and supported almost everywhere.

The period between 1378 and 1417 is known as the Great Western Schism, but it is far from being the only time when there was more than one pope. In fact, there have been a great number of antipopes down the centuries, all of whom managed to attract significant support from cardinals, and exercise real influence. Any other claimants who failed to gain such support and power, are not deemed to have technically been 'antipopes'; they instead are known by the confusing term 'Sedevacantist antipopes'. The first recognised antipope was Hippolytus, who died in the year 235 AD. Hippolytus had led a rival faction within the Roman Church, in protest against Pope Callixtus I. The next antipope was Novatian, who died in 258, after claiming the papacy in opposition to Pope Cornelius. In total there have been at least 38 antipopes in the intervening years, with most occurring between the 10th and 12th centuries.

As you might expect, the Catholic Church today has a clear view about which past popes were legitimate, and which were antipopes, even if the matter was less clear at the time, and this official list of popes is called the *Annuario Pontificio*. However, what is particularly interesting is that even the Vatican seems to be unable to make a clear ruling in every case, and so even the Church's official list suggests that at certain times there was more than one valid pope, even though of course this is impossible, in theological terms. For example, Pope Silverius was forced to resign by his successor, Vigilius, but according to the *Annuario Pontificio*, Silverius didn't resign until November 11, 537, some months after Vigilius's election on March 29, 537. Two popes can't hold office simultaneously, so one of these must have been an antipope, but the records don't distinguish. Similarly, Pope Martin I died in exile in 655, having never resigned. However, at the time no one in Rome knew whether he would make it back, or even if he was still alive, and so they elected his replacement Pope Eugenius I in 654, which again means that there were two simultaneous, valid popes.

There is even a current antipope today. The Palmarian Catholic Church is a rival schism, which claims that a series of apparitions have proven that the Roman See has been excommunicated since 1978, with the authority transferring to the See of El Palmar de Troya. In 2005, the Palmarians elected a successor to their Pope Gregory XVII, who had ruled since 1978. As a result, the current Palmarian pope, or antipope, is Manuel Alonso Corral, who also goes by the title of Pope Peter II, in opposition to the more widely accepted Pope Benedict XVI of Rome.

What went wrong on Easter Island?

Easter Island is thought to be the loneliest scrap of habitable land on the planet. The island measures just 63 square miles, and its nearest inhabited neighbour is Pitcairn Island, 1,289 miles to the west, which has just a few hundred inhabitants. Easter Island's nearest neighbour to the east is Chile, 2,180 miles away. Despite its remote location, Easter Island has been inhabited for possibly as long as 1,600 years. At one time, it had a thriving society, and yet by the time European explorers arrived in the early 18th century, the island was a barren, thinly populated wasteland. So what had happened to cause the society of Easter Island to collapse so dramatically?

The first European to set eyes on Easter Island was the Dutch explorer Jacob Roggeveen, who named it after spotting it on Easter Day in 1722. He was baffled by the island, for two reasons. Firstly, it was not clear how the Easter Islanders could have got there in the first place. The canoes of the current Easter Islanders were small, leaky craft made of thin planks strung together with thread – these canoes could never have crossed the vast oceans required to reach the island. Secondly, the island was littered with enormous stone statues, the famous Easter Island heads, which were up to ten metres in height, and weighed as much as 80 tons. The island was a place of 'singular poverty and barrenness', Roggeveen wrote, with no trees, no ropes, and no timber to be found anywhere. With no timber and no ropes, how could the islanders have possibly built the necessary tools and machinery to produce and transport these enormous statues?

The answer seems to be that the Easter Islanders had once had all of these things: timber, rope, and tools, along with a thriving society, but they had destroyed their own habitat, in a tragic and superstitious arms race. Hundreds of years beforehand, the island had been a lush, sub-tropical paradise, covered with dense forest, with a rich assortment of wildlife. The islanders had eaten a varied diet, including porpoises and dolphins which they harpooned at sea, and many varieties of seabird which nested in the forest.

However, as the population grew, there was increasing pressure on the land. This was exacerbated by the island-ers' strange ritual of building enormous stone heads, known as 'Maoi', which are thought to have functioned as a tribute to their ancestors, or their gods. Producing these huge stat-ues used up considerable resources, as massive quantities of timber and rope were needed to produce, transport, and mount the statues, which were positioned around the island's coast, facing inwards, as if watching over the island, and pro-tecting the islanders from harm.

At some point, the island's population may have reached as much as 20,000, but by the time the Europeans arrived, it had dropped to just 2,000. It seems that, as the population had grown, more and more of the forest had been destroyed, to be used as fuel, to free up land for farming, and to produce increasingly large Maoi. As the forest shrank, there were fewer trees for the seabirds to nest in, which meant there were fewer seabirds, which had been a key part of the islanders' diet, and may have played an important role in pollinating the trees' flowers, and dispersing their fruit.

As the process continued, the native birds died out, and food shortages increased. Around the year 1500, porpoise seems to have disappeared from the islanders' diet, because there were no more trees of the right size or species to pro-duce timber and rope for the kind of large seagoing canoes that were needed to hunt porpoises. With no forests left, the soil was easily eroded by rain and wind, and baked by the sun.

A society which had once been organised and centralised now disintegrated into tribal warfare and cannibalism, with people living in caves for their own safety.

One of the saddest aspects of this story is perhaps the role of the islanders' supernatural belief in the Maoi. When the Europeans arrived, they found an astonishing 200 statues mounted around the coast, with another 700 in varying states of completeness. It seems that, as the food supplies had grown shorter each year, the islanders had believed that the solution would be to create ever-greater tributes to their gods, instead of trying to preserve and manage their habitat. As each year's famine turned out to be worse than the last, the islanders must have resolved each time to tear down more of the forest, to produce larger and larger Maoi, desperate to do whatever it would take to appease the cruel gods who continued to punish them.

Why did the Xhosa people of South Africa slaughter all their cattle?

In 1856, something strange happened among the Xhosa nation of what is the now the Eastern Cape province of South Africa. Because of a shared delusion, the community began killing all of their cattle, and destroying all of their crops, after a young girl prophesied that if they did so, they would be rewarded by the spirits. Amazingly, this outlandish story took hold, in what seems to have been a senseless outbreak of mass hysteria, and the Xhosa people willingly went ahead and destroyed all of their food.

The story began in the most innocent way. Two young girls went out to scare off the birds in the cornfields near the River Gxara. When they returned to the kraal, one of the girls, whose name was Nongqawuse, told her uncle that she had seen three spirits in the bushes, who had told her that the tribe should slaughter all of their cattle, and destroy all of their crops. If they did this, the spirits would return, and provide great numbers of even more beautiful cattle; huge swathes of new crops would instantly appear, and the British settlers who were threatening the community would be driven off the Xhosa lands.

Nongqawuse's uncle Mhlakaza was known to be a prophet himself, and so when he told people that he believed his niece's visions, they felt they should take them seriously. The clan's Paramount Chief Sarhili was initially sceptical, but after a time he too became convinced, and ordered that the spirits' commands be obeyed. The community now divided into believers and non-believers, but as pressure grew on the non-believers, they too were forced to destroy their food. Soon, more than 300,000 cattle had been slaughtered, along with many acres of valuable corn. Meanwhile, the people prepared enormous, empty livestock enclosures, ready to hold all the new cattle that were coming, and huge containers made of animal skins, to hold the vast quantities of milk that had been promised.

Nongqawuse had prophesied that on 18 February 1857, the sun would be red when it rose in the morning, and the spirits would fulfil their promise. However on the day of judgement, the sunrise was the same colour as always, and nothing happened. At first the people blamed the non-believers, suspecting that not enough cattle had been slaughtered to appease the spirits, but they soon turned on Nongqawuse and her uncle. Sarili pointed at Nogqawuse and said, 'The reason we are broken today is on account of this girl.'

A dreadful famine soon followed, with as many as 70-80,000 Xhosa tribespeople dying, out of a population of just 105,000. In desperation, people tried to boil and eat their ox-hide shields and leather skirts. Some collapsed and died just yards from the soup kitchens provided by the British, too weak to take the final steps. There were even reports of some turning to cannibalism. And of course, the starving community were in no position to defend themselves from the British settlers, and were soon conquered and assimilated into the colony. And what became of Nogqawuse herself? She was arrested by the British, and imprisoned on the notorious Robben Island.

How did animal fat almost cost Britain her Empire?

India was known as the 'Jewel in the Crown' of the British Empire, as India's wealth was pillaged, and used to help Britain amass the largest empire the world had ever seen. By 1922, the British Empire covered almost a quarter of the world's land surface, more than 13 million square miles, and controlled more than a quarter of the world's population, with more than 450 million subjects. India was both Britain's most populous and most valuable colony, generating enormous revenues for the East India Company through trade and taxation, and yet the 'Jewel in the Crown' was almost lost in 1857, over what should have been a minor dispute concerning animal fats.

The issue that sparked the Indian Mutiny was the introduction of the new Enfield rifle, to replace the inaccurate, smooth-bore muskets which had previously been issued to the native soldiers of the Indian Army, who were known as *sepoys*. To load the muskets, soldiers would ram the bullet and some loose gunpowder down the long barrel using a ramrod. The new rifles, on the other hand, would be much more accurate, and could be easily loaded using a new kind of paper-coated cartridge, which contained both the bullet and the precise amount of gunpowder. The sepoys would simply have to bite off the end of the paper, and push the cartridge down the barrel.

The new rifles ought to have been a welcome advance, but there was one problem. The cartridges had to be heavily greased, for ease of loading, and it hadn't occurred to the British that the grease they had chosen to use, which was pork fat and beef fat, might be problematic. Of course, as the sepoys began to hear about the new cartridges, the Muslims among them were deeply offended by the prospect of having to bite on pork fat, while the Hindus were equally outraged by the beef fat, as cows are sacred to the Hindu faith. When these concerns were raised by the sepoys, they were dismissed and ignored by the British, even though alternatives such as sheep fat, goat fat, or vegetable oil could all have been easily substituted, without a significant increase in cost.

The issue was exacerbated because it played to other fears that had been growing among the native population. In particular, Indians were increasingly afraid that Britain was planning to forcibly convert them to Christianity. In its early years, the East India Company had seemed to have no interest in anything but money, and had shown no inclination to interfere in India's cultural or religious life. However, the new wave of young officers arriving from Britain seemed to be different. Many of them were evangelical Christians, who openly attempted to convert the Indians, even though the Company itself specifically advised against this. This new breed of officers were also more likely to be short-term careerists, hoping to move quickly from the army into a better-paid civilian post. This meant they had little interest in getting to know the sepoys under their command, unlike the earlier, more adventurous class of British officers, who had been more likely to share the hardships and dangers of their sepoy comrades, and taken trouble to learn the native language and customs.

Despite the sepoys' fears, there was no reason why the conflict should have escalated, except for British arrogance and incompetence. The East India Company allowed ludicrous rumours to spread, including the claim that powdered pig-bones and cow-bones were being added to the Indians' flour, that Britain had been defeated in the Crimean War, and that eligible Indian men would be forced to marry the widows of English soldiers. When the sepoys complained about the cartridges, the British were instructed to force the issue, and to treat any resistance as mutiny, to be punished by court-martial. The Commander-in-Chief in India, General the Honourable George Anson declared, 'I'll never give in to their beastly prejudices.'

The issue was also intensified because of a mysterious prophecy which seems to have taken root, a belief that British rule in India would fall after exactly 100 years. This crisis took place in 1857, exactly 100 years after Britain's decisive victory at the Battle of Plassey. The coded message 'Sub lal hogea hai', meaning 'everything has become red' began to circulate, and people began to distribute lotus flowers and chapatis (a small unleavened flatbread) from town to town and village to village, which seem to have symbolised the same message. The origins of the code may be unclear, but the message was not: the days of subjugation were over, and the Firangis would soon be killed.

The crisis erupted in Meerut, in northern India. Here and elsewhere, the sepoys had taken a solemn oath not to touch the cartridges, and many British officers had had the good sense not to provoke a futile and dangerous confrontation.

However, Colonel George Carmichael-Smyth, commander of the 3rd Indian Light Cavalry took a different view, and assembled his men on the parade ground, and demanded they each take out three cartridges. All but five refused, which meant Carmichael-Smyth now had no option but to court-martial the 90 rebels, with most of them being sentenced to ten years' hard labour.

A few weeks' later, the prisoners were punished on the parade ground, in front of the company of 4,000 men. Their legs were shackled, their gold buttons were cut off, and their uniforms were ripped up the back, before they were marched away in disgrace. The next day, the sepoys rioted, and much of the city of Meerut was set on fire. That night, more than fifty Europeans, including men, women, and children, were hacked to death, as the city exploded into violence, and the anarchy soon spread to much of northern India. As the so-called 'mutiny' escalated, there were dreadful massacres in many cities, and it took fourteen months of sustained fighting to eventually regain control.

8
EXTRAORDINARY EPISODES

'History... just one damned thing after another.'
Arnold Toynbee (1889-1975)

What caused the spear tips of Julius Caesar's army to burn with a blue flame?

In his account of the Gallic Wars, *Commentarii de Bello Gallico*, Julius Caesar describes a strange event which took place after a hailstorm, and caused considerable consternation among the soldiers of the Fifth Legion: 'In the month of February, about the second watch of the night, there suddenly arose a thick cloud followed by a shower of hail, and the same night the points of the spears belonging to the Fifth Legion seem to take fire.'

In fact, what the army were witnessing was a strange electrical phenomenon which is known as St Elmo's Fire, in which small blue or violet flames appear to burn from the top of pointed structures such as masts or steeples, sometimes accompanied by a hissing or crackling sound. Although St Elmo's Fire is more likely to be seen on tall structures such as masts, streetlamps, and towers, it can sometimes be seen on the horns of cattle, or even on the corners of certain types of hat. St Elmo's Fire occurs most often after a storm, when there is a high electrical charge in the air.

The cause of St Elmo's Fire is somewhat similar to lightning, in that it is caused by there being a difference between the electrical charge of the air beneath a thunderstorm and the ground. In the case of St Elmo's Fire, the difference in charge between a tall object such as a mast or church steeple and the surrounding air causes the air to become ionised and spark, emitting a constant blue glow. This process of ionisation is the same effect as that which occurs inside a neon tube, the key difference being that neon produces an orange glow, while oxygen and nitrogen – the main elements of our atmosphere – glow blue.

Historians as far back as Pliny the Elder have written with awe about this strange phenomenon, which was also witnessed by many great explorers including Ferdinand Magellan and Christopher Columbus. Charles Darwin described witnessing the strange glow while onboard The Beagle, 'Everything is in flames, - the sky with lightning, - the water with luminous particles, and even the very masts are pointed with a blue flame.' It was also seen during the Muslim Siege of Constantinople in 1453. The Byzantines believed it to be a sign of God's providence, but days later the city fell, bringing the Byzantine Empire to an end.

The phenomenon is named St Elmo's Fire after the patron saint of Mediterranean sailors, who is known to us as St Erasmus, but to Italians as St Elmo. Although St Elmo's Fire can occur on land, it was historically most often seen at sea, for the simple reason that, until fairly recently, ships tended to be the tallest structures around, before multi-storey buildings became viable. Because it was generally seen at sea, sailors tended to attribute mystical significance to the phenomenon, usually regarding it as a sign of good luck, or a guiding light for lost ships. Presumably, the fact that St Elmo's Fire tends to occur at the end of a storm, rather than the beginning, encouraged the perception that it was a positive omen.

Why did Count Robert of Anjou come to regret his confidence in 866?

From the late 8th century onwards, any part of northern Europe accessible by sea or river was now under threat from the marauding Vikings, including the areas now known as northern France, the Low Countries, and Germany. The churches and towns of West Francia (present-day France, broadly speaking) were frequently sacked from around 840 onwards, with the Vikings only agreeing to return home when enough bribes or loot had been collected to satisfy them, usually in the form of precious metals. Paris was looted in 845, when Vikings sailed their longboats up the Seine, and then three more times during the 860s.

In 864, the King of West Francia, Charles the Bald, issued the Edict of Pistres, which consisted of a number of measures to defend the region from the Vikings. Every man who owned or could afford a horse was required to serve in the newly-formed cavalry, to create a powerful, mobile force. There were strict new penalties for anyone caught trading with the Vikings: the punishment for selling them a horse was death. Additionally, every town was required to build fortified bridges, to prevent Vikings sailing their longboats inland.

The region surrounding Paris was ruled by Count Robert of Anjou, also known as Robert the Strong, who in 862 had won a famous victory against the Vikings, capturing twelve of their ships, and killing everyone onboard. In 866, Robert had to defend the region from a joint attack, as the Vikings joined forces with Robert's enemy, Salomon, Duke of Brittany. The raiders sacked Le Mans, and moved deep into the Anjou region. Robert raised a large army in response, and intercepted the attackers on land, at Brissarthe, before they could reach their ships on the River Loire. The Vikings took refuge in a church, under siege from Robert and his army.

However, it was at this point that Robert made his fatal mistake. With the insurgents besieged, he took off his armour and helmet, presumably to take a rest from carrying their hefty weight. Suddenly, the Vikings burst out of the church and attacked, killing the defenceless Robert in the process, and wounding the Franks' other significant leader, Ranulf, Duke of Aquitaine. The Frankish army was now in disarray, with no leaders, and as panic set in, they quickly scattered, and the Vikings were allowed to escape.

How did a single arrow change the course of England's history?

The Battle of Hastings marked a momentous shift in English history. The Anglo-Saxon nobility was wiped out, as William divided the nation among his Norman supporters, who became the new nobility. William also changed the landscape of England, building a great number of castles, forts, and keeps, including the Tower of London, and these, along with his piecemeal division of land, limited the possibilities of rebellion, and consolidated the power of the monarchy. William was an effective administrator, who strengthened the function of England's shires and institutions, and improved the tax system after compiling the Domesday Book, an unprecedented survey of the nation's population and resources. The

Anglo-Saxon culture came to merge with that of Normandy and France, making a significant contribution to the English language, as the language of the nobility was now Norman French, and this soon filtered down into every level of society.

One interesting example of this was the way in which animals continued to be known by their Anglo-Saxon names, such as cow, pig, and sheep, whereas meat came to be known by French words: beef (from the French word 'boeuf'), pork ('porc'), and mutton ('mouton'). The obvious explanation for this divide is that animals were still generally farmed by the Anglo-Saxon peasants, and so retained their old names, whereas meat was generally only eaten by the Norman nobility, and so it came to be known by Norman words.

William's victory at the Battle of Hastings had a profound effect on the future of England, but it could so nearly have been very different. The battle was closely fought, and the two sides were evenly matched, with around 7,000-8,000 troops each. Contemporary battles tended only to last for a couple of hours at most, but the Battle of Hastings went on all day, for around 9 hours, which reflected both the closeness of the fight, and the determination of both armies. William had given a rousing speech before the battle promising his army that the spoils of England would be divided among them if they were victorious. Harold's army was equally resolute, as the core of it was made up of professional soldiers known as Housecarls, who were renowned for their loyalty to the king.

For most of the day, there was little to divide the two armies. King Harold had secured a dominant, elevated position on Senlac Hill above the isthmus, and there he set up his forces in a defensive position. The Norman army was a more versatile force, being comprised of archers and cavalry as well as infantry, while Harold's army was solely made up of foot soldiers. However, Harold's effective use of closely formed shield walls succeeded in nullifying the Norman archers, and as long as the English maintained their tight, defensive formation, the French cavalry would be largely ineffective.

As dusk fell, an English victory seemed all but assured. Battles were not fought at night, so once the sun set, the armies would have to return to their camps and regroup. However, Harold was certain to gain significant reinforcements in the morning, while William had no more resources to draw upon, and was trapped along the shore. With perhaps as little as half an hour of the battle left, William made what may have been the decisive call. Seeing that Harold's shield wall was now significantly depleted, with only the front ranks holding shields, he ordered his archers to fire their arrows into the air, over the front lines, and into the massed, unprotected troops behind. As arrows rained down, the English army began to splinter, and King Harold was struck by an arrow in the eye, which killed him. With no leader, the English army fell into disarray, with many of them fleeing the field, and William had won the key battle of the Norman Conquest.

In medieval times, why did spiral staircases usually wind clockwise?

If you visit any surviving medieval castle, you will generally find that any spiral staircase will usually wind clockwise, from the point of view of the person ascending. The simple reason for this is that a clockwise ascent puts any sword-wielding attacker at a disadvantage, when faced with a defender coming down the stairs. To take a decent swing, a swordsman coming up the stairs would have to expose all of his body to the defender, and would still be likely to be hampered by the central column.

This assumes of course that both fighters are right-handed, which is not an unreasonable assumption. In fact, swords have historically been designed to be asymmetrical, meaning that they can only be used effectively by one particular hand, and so left-handed swords are rare. It seems therefore that medieval soldiers would have been trained to fight right-handed, even if they were naturally lefties.

How was Robert the Bruce inspired by a spider?

It is a strange fact that Scotland's most celebrated national hero seems to be William Wallace, who was immortalised in the film *Braveheart*, rather than Robert the Bruce, despite the fact that the main difference between them is arguably that Robert the Bruce succeeded where Wallace had failed. They were both wealthy landowners, as well as being great warriors. The two men were contemporaries, who both fought for Scottish independence against the English, although there is no record of them ever fighting together on the same side. And yet, despite their similarities, it is Wallace who is most revered in Scotland, even though he was captured in 1305, and brutally executed, while Robert the Bruce was crowned King of Scots in 1306, and defeated England's Edward II in the decisive Battle of Bannockburn in 1314.

The most likely reason for Wallace's pre-eminence is that he never fought on the side of the English, whereas Robert the Bruce did. As one of Scotland's leading landowners, Bruce was one of the two leading claimants for the Scots' throne, along with John Comyn. During the late 1290s, Bruce sometimes fought on the side of the Scots, and sometimes with the English, against his rival. The turning point is said to have been a celebratory meal after an English victory. Bruce sat eating alongside his English comrades, with blood still on his hands from the battle. At this point, two English lords began to mock him, saying, 'Look at that Scotsman, who is eating his own blood!'. From this point on, Bruce never again fought against his own countrymen.

As King Edward I's power in Scotland grew, in 1305 Bruce offered Comyn a deal: either Comyn could forfeit his claim to the throne, and in return Bruce would give him all his lands, or alternatively Bruce would give up the crown, and receive Comyn's lands in return. Comyn decided to take the land, and so Bruce's path to the throne was now clear. However, at this point Comyn seems to have double-crossed Bruce, revealing their secret pact to Edward I. When Bruce confronted Comyn about this treachery, in the Church of Greyfriars in Dumfries, the two men came to blows, and Comyn was killed, either by Bruce himself or his two attendants. For the sacrilege of killing in a church Bruce was now excommunicated, and his situation became increasingly desperate.

Bruce now gathered together a band of followers, and had himself crowned King of Scots at the Abbey of Scone. However, soon afterwards he was defeated by the English at the Battle of Methven, and briefly captured. After yet another defeat soon after, Bruce was forced to go on the run, to Rathlin Island off the northern coast of Ireland. There, Bruce was hiding one night in a wooden hut, when he noticed a spider in the beams above him, dangling from a long thread which it had spun. Repeatedly, the spider tried to swing itself from one roof beam to another, to fix a line on which it could build its web, but each time it failed. Bruce counted six attempts, and then realised that, coincidentally, he had lost six battles to the English. He now decided that if the spider succeeded with its seventh attempt, he would persevere with the fight in Scotland, but if it failed, he would go off to Palestine to join the Crusades. This time, the spider made it across, and so Bruce decided that he too would persevere and fight on.

In July 1307, Edward I died, and the crown passed to his son, who became King Edward II (the same Edward II who had an unpleasant encounter with a red hot poker in Chapter Four). Unlike his father, Edward II was not much of a warrior, and seemed to have little interest in Scotland. Bruce returned to Scotland, and over the next few years captured a number of English-held castles, using novel guerrilla tactics, and refusing to meet the English in open battle. Bruce gradually gained control of Scotland, until in the spring of 1314, Edward II was forced to ride north to raise the siege on the strategically important castle at Stirling. In the battle that followed at Bannockburn, Scotland's armies were outnumbered by around 3 to 1, but Robert the Bruce won a famous victory, by carefully selecting a boggy, uneven battleground, which thwarted the English cavalry.

There is one other strange story concerning Robert the Bruce, regarding his heart. Before his death, Bruce requested that his heart should be removed from his body, and then taken to battle in a Crusade. This was apparently motivated by his own failure to go on a Crusade, as well as his desire to observe penance for murdering John Comyn in the Church of Greyfriars. Bruce's request was honoured, as Sir James Douglas placed the king's heart in a silver casket, and prepared to take it to war. When plans for a new international Crusade came to nothing, Douglas sailed to Spain to fight the Moors instead, and was killed in battle in 1330 at the siege of Teba. In 1996, archaeologists discovered a silver casket while carrying out building work at Melrose Abbey in Roxburghshire, and found that, as suspected, it did indeed contain a human heart.

What became of Lambert Simnel?

When Henry VII took the English throne in 1485, emerging victorious from the thirty-year Wars of the Roses, the nobility was still largely divided into Yorkist and Lancastrian factions. This divide was at the heart of the first major challenge to Henry's reign, when in 1487 there appeared a young boy who claimed to be the true king of England. Rumours had been circulating that the Princes in the Tower, the two sons of King Edward IV, had not in fact been murdered, but were still alive. This boy claimed to be the younger of the two, Edward, Earl of Warwick, and as such he was a Yorkist pretender to the throne.

In fact, the boy was an impostor, who had been coached and trained by an ambitious cleric from Oxford named Roger Simons. The boy is known today by the name Lambert Simnel, but both his first name and surname may well have been false, as records are sketchy, and both names were very unusual for the time. As a child, Simnel was taken on as a pupil by Simons, who had noticed that the true way to advancement in this society was not by hard work, but by patronage. If Simons could somehow win the favour of someone powerful, he might be given a bishopric, or perhaps even the archbishopric of Canterbury. Noticing that Simnel was unusually good looking, Simons decided to train him in etiquette and courtly manners, so that he could be presented as one of the two Princes in the Tower. At first, the plan was to claim that Simnel was Richard, Duke of York, but at some point Simons decided to claim Simnel as Edward, Earl of Warwick instead.

As rumours spread that Edward had escaped from the Tower, leading Yorkists rallied around the cause, including Margaret, Dowager Duchess of Burgundy, and the Earl of Lincoln. Many of them seem not to have actually believed that Simnel was really Edward, but it didn't really matter; the point was to put a Yorkist on the throne, who could then be either controlled or got rid of. The Yorkists managed to raise an army of 2,000 Flemish mercenaries, and then travelled to Ireland, where the boy was crowned King Edward VI at Christ Church Cathedral in Dublin.

Lambert Simnel's army was now ready to invade England, and landed near Furness in Lancashire on 5th June 1487. The Yorkists hoped to swell their army by adding English supporters, but after thirty years of civil war, the locals seem to have had no appetite for further conflict, particularly when the invading army comprised mostly Irish and Flemish troops. The Yorkists eventually met Henry's army at the Battle of Stoke Field on 16th June, but the King's well-trained, well-armed forces easily defeated Simnel's disorganised rabble. Some of the leading rebels were killed, including the Earl of Lincoln. Simons was imprisoned, and probably spared execution only because he was a member of the clergy.

Henry was also urged to execute Lambert Simnel, the impostor who had been the focus of the rebellion, but instead he decided to take pity on him. Like many before him, Henry was charmed by the intelligent, well mannered boy, and recognised that he had been merely a pawn in the conspiracy. As a result, rather than executing him, he instead gave him a job cooking and washing pots in the royal kitchens. Later, Simnel rose through the ranks of the royal household, becoming Henry's falconer. It's not clear when Lambert Simnel died, but he is known to have been alive as late as 1534.

How did a boatload of peat win back the city of Breda for the Dutch?

In 1581, the Dutch city of Breda was conquered by the Spanish army, in what was an important victory of the Eighty Years' War, which is also known as the Dutch War of Independance. The Spanish had managed to enter the walled city by bribing a sentry to open the castle gates. With the castle lost, the citizens of Breda offered to surrender without a fight, in return for a ceasefire, but the Spanish showed no mercy, and a massacre ensued, in which 584 citizens were killed. As a result of this atrocity, Breda became an important symbol for the Dutch, and they were therefore determined to retake the stronghold.

However, Breda was a heavily fortified, walled city, which seemed to be impregnable. The Dutch kept it under siege, but there seemed little hope of meaningful progress, until a young man named Adriaen van Bergen came up with an idea. Van Bergen was the owner of a boat which the Spanish allowed to regularly bring peat into the city. According to van Bergen, the Spanish soldiers never inspected his boat, because it was filled with smelly peat (peat is essentially damp, rotting vegetation, which can be used as fuel). Van Bergen thus proposed to the leader of the Dutch army, Prince Maurice of Nassau, that the peat boat could be used as a kind of Trojan horse, to sneak a small armed force into the city.

Prince Maurice approved the idea, and so plans were set in motion, but on the day of departure, van Bergen went missing, claiming to have overslept, and so the operation was delayed. The next day, van Bergen pulled out altogether, having apparently lost his nerve, and sent his two nephews in his place. Despite this, the mission went ahead, with 70 Dutch soldiers concealed in the boat which was piled high with peat. Maurice had decided that the soldiers should remain hidden for the entire voyage, to avoid arousing suspicion, but the river became blocked with ice, which meant the men had to spend four days trapped in the cramped, stinking conditions.

Eventually the ice cleared, and the boat reached Breda Castle. As predicted, the Spanish showed little interest in inspecting the boat, but the plan was almost scuppered when the barge suddenly sprang a leak. As the hidden soldiers frantically pumped to try and clear out the water, the Spanish troops actually helped to rescue the boat, by tying it to the quay in such a way that the damage was above the waterline. The Dutch soldiers now remained hidden until nightfall, before finally climbing out of their soggy, stinking hiding place, and retaking the castle. They now opened the castle gates for the rest of Maurice's army, and Breda was once again in Dutch hands, thanks to what Dutch history remembers as the *Turfschip van Breda*.

Why did Pope Urban VIII ban the taking of snuff?

Snuff is a tobacco product which is made by grinding tobacco leaves into a fine powder, which users sniff into their nostrils. Europeans first observed the practice on Haiti, during Columbus's second journey to the Americas in 1493-6. Over the 16th century, the habit became popular among the wealthy, thanks in part to the support of Catherine de Medici, who believed that snuff offered a range of health benefits, and used it to treat her son's persistent migraines.

By the 17th century, the habit had spread, with reports of snuff use as far afield as China. There were all sorts of bizarre claims for the effects of snuff, including that it could cure colds, migraine, sinus and tooth pain, asthma, constipation, and even correct poor eyesight. King Louis XIII of France was a keen snuff-taker, and the habit was perceived as being a mark of the elite and wealthy, as the lower classes would generally smoke their tobacco. Snuff also had an appealing range of elaborate and luxurious paraphernalia, with ornate pocket snuff boxes (for daily use) made of horn, and larger snuff containers called 'mulls' (for storage at home) decorated with silver. Even today there is a lavish silver communal snuff box at the entrance to the House of Commons.

So, if snuff was favoured by the wealthy and powerful, why would the Pope of all people disapprove? The answer is that Pope Urban VIII had a bizarre hatred of sneezing, which he believed to be closely related to orgasms, and therefore sinful and immoral. Snuff often makes its users sneeze, which presumably means the Pope regarded it as a kind of dangerous sexual stimulant. Amazingly, he issued a papal bull threatening to excommunicate anyone caught taking snuff.

Who was 58th in line for the British throne after the death of Queen Anne?

The answer is George Lewis, the Elector of Hanover, who was a German aristocrat. The significance of this question is that, despite there apparently being 57 people with a better claim to the British throne than George, it was George who took it, becoming the first in a line of Hanoverian kings. The frail and sickly Queen Anne had sadly failed to produce any heir who survived beyond infancy, despite undergoing 18 pregnancies. As a result, despite his lowly position in the hereditary order of succession, George was handed the crown by Parliament, for the simple reason that, unlike the other, superior claimants, he wasn't a Catholic.

Consequently, on 18 September 1714, George sailed up the River Thames to land at Greenwich, before being crowned King George I a month later at Westminster Abbey. However, although the majority of Englishmen approved of George's religion, or at least approved of the king not being a Catholic, George was seen to have few other qualities. He was a short, charmless, and grumpy 54 year old. He took an unprecedented, austere approach to kingship, refusing to take part in any of the proper pomp and ceremony expected of a monarch. He had an openly hostile relationship with his son, which would become a Hanoverian tradition, and he had imprisoned his own wife before his accession, and may also have had her Swedish lover killed.

Most importantly, George was very clearly German, with no affection for England or the English. Of course, England had fairly recent experience of foreign leaders, after the Glorious Revolution had brought William III to the throne, but William was not nearly as foreign as George. William spoke fluent English, had an English mother, and had married an English princess. After taking the throne, he had lived in England, and devoted his energies to England. As a result, Britain had quickly been allowed to overtake William's native Dutch Republic to become the world's leading financial and naval power.

George, on the other hand, was born in Germany, to German parents, spoke no English, and had no interest in learning any. He arrived with German ministers, German bodyguards, and German mistresses. After his coronation, he spent as much time as possible in Hanover, as little time as possible in England, and took little interest in English affairs. At first, he did attempt to attend cabinet meetings, but required the use of a translator, as he could not understand what was being said. Eventually, he gave up, and largely left the running of Britain to First Lord of the Treasury Robert Walpole, while he focussed his energies on Hanover, where he could wield more effective, autocratic power. As a result, Walpole is regarded as having been Britain's first Prime Minister, although there was no such official position or title at the time, and in fact 'prime minister' at the time was considered an insulting term, which Walpole rejected.

As a result, George was deeply unpopular from the start, with mocking banners being displayed around the country even on the day of his coronation. The general election of 1715 was a violent one, with banners condemning George and the Hanoverian succession. Later that year George faced a major uprising, the Jacobite Rebellion, as a 20,000 strong Scottish army led by the Earl of Mar attempted to place a Stuart king on the throne, before being defeated by George's forces.

Who were The Elephant and The Maypole?

This question follows on from the last one, as 'The Elephant and The Maypole' were the cruel public nicknames given to King George I's two notoriously unattractive mistresses, as one was said to be short and fat, while the other was tall and thin. George's wife Sophia had been imprisoned for adultery, which was a bit rich given that her affair had only begun after the boorish George had consistently ignored her, preferring to spend time with his own various mistresses. Sophia is said to have been a pretty and engaging young woman, but George had her incarcerated at the age of just 28, and she would spend the rest of her life in jail, never again to see her two young children.

So, with his wife behind bars at the Castle of Ahlden, George arrived in England with his two mistresses, who were soon dubbed with their unfortunate nicknames. The first was the tall, thin Melusine von der Schulenburg, who bore George at least three illegitimate children, and was described by the effective Prime Minister Robert Walpole as being 'as much the Queen of England as anyone was'.

The second was the short, round Sophia von Kielmansegg, who was the illegitimate daughter of Ernest Augustus, the former Elector of Hanover. Ernest Augustus also happened to be George's father, thus making Sophia the King's half-sister, but it's not clear whether this means that the rumours that she was also the King's mistress were false. When George gave her the titles of Countess of Leinster, Countess of Darlington, and Baroness Brentford, the letters patent described her as 'of our common blood', and her coat of arms included the arms of Brunswick with a bar sinister, a heraldic device indicating that she was an illegitimate daughter of an Elector of Hanover.

What was the South Sea Bubble?

As the global economy continues to struggle to recover from the effects of the housing boom and resulting credit crunch, it may be reassuring to learn that financial meltdowns of this type are nothing new, and have occurred a number of times throughout history. One of the earliest incidences of speculative mania was the South Sea Bubble, which almost bankrupted the Bank of England in the 18th century.

The British had watched enviously over the preceding two centuries, as Britain's hated enemy Spain had grown rich from the gold and silver mines of Mexico and Peru. In 1711, as hostilities with Spain seemed to be coming to an end, the South

Sea Company was formed, with the intention of trading with South America. When the War of Spanish Succession ended in 1713, the South Sea Company was granted monopoly rights to trade with South America, and investors began imagining great profits, as English goods such as wool and fleece would be traded for treasure chests filled with South American gold and silver. The South Sea Company was publicly supported and endorsed by many of the nobility, including royalty and Members of Parliament, and investors clamoured to come onboard, as the stock price soared higher and higher, at one point trebling in value in a single day.

However, the company's prospects were not quite as rosy as they appeared. The agreement with Spain only allowed the company to bring one ship to South America per year, carrying a cargo of not more than 500 tons, which meant potential profits were strictly limited. Also, the idea that South America was craving English woollen goods and knick-knacks was plainly daft. In fact, over the following years, the South Sea Company would struggle to make a profit from any kind of trade except for slaves, in which it was moderately successful.

The South Sea Company was less focussed on delivering the promised profits than on what seem to have been its real goals: enriching the shareholders, and taking on government debt. This first goal was partly achieved by the involvement of many of the great and the good, including King George I himself, which gave the company respectability and prestige, encouraging smaller investors to rush to subscribe. MPs and lords were given shares and, crucially, share options, on extremely favourable terms, which meant they all had a vested financial interest in driving up the share price, by spreading absurd stories about the company's prospects and successes.

The company's second role was to manage government debt. The company managed to persuade holders of government bonds to exchange them for South Sea Company shares, which meant the company was effectively taking on a significant chunk of Britain's national debt. In return, the government paid the Company a healthy rate of interest, making it a win-win situation for everyone, except of course the investors. By 1719, the company had taken on £31 million of Britain's £50 million national debt.

As the public demand for South Sea stock grew, a huge number of other 'joint-stock' companies were launched, with many making ridiculous and fraudulent claims for their future prospects. One company planned to produce square cannon balls. Another proposed to increase Britain's land mass by building floating mansions. Yet another was famously advertised as 'a company for carrying out an undertaking of great advantage, but nobody to know what it is.' Many of these so-called 'bubble' companies would barely last a week, before disappearing with their investors' money, and so in response Parliament passed the Bubble Act in June 1720, banning all joint-stock companies except those approved by Parliament or Royal Charter. This gave a further boost to the South Sea Company, whose share price now soared even higher, reaching £1,000 in early August.

At this point, the bubble burst, as investors began rushing to sell. There are a number of possible explanations for why the bubble suddenly burst. There were rumours that Sir John Blunt, the governor of the Company, and the other directors had sold their shares, which undermined public confidence. A price of £1,000 may have been a psychologically important milestone, encouraging holders to sell, or dissuading potential buyers. Some investors may have finally seen that the share price was unjustifiably high, and tried to cash in their profits. Another possible reason is that August was the first due date for many investors to pay the first instalment on their shares, which had been bought on credit, credit provided by the South Sea Company itself. Since many of these people had no money, the only way they could pay for their shares was to sell them.

By September, the crisis had become international, as other similar schemes collapsed, including John Law's 'Mississippi Scheme', which had planned to convert France's monetary system from gold and silver to paper currency. The South Sea Company's share price dropped to £150, and many investors were ruined, including the composer George Frideric Handel. Five established English banks collapsed, and there was even a run on the Bank of England. Parliament began an investigation, and many MPs were impeached, with Chancellor of the Exchequer John Aislabie sensationally imprisoned in the Tower of London. However, despite causing financial ruin for many, the South Sea Company amazingly continued to operate, continuing even into the reign of Queen Victoria.

Why were the royal clocks at Sandringham always kept half an hour fast?

Sandringham is a country estate in Norfolk, England, and one of the royal family's favourite residences. Britain's monarchs have owned Sandringham House since 1862, when it was bought by Queen Victoria for her son, the future Edward VII, who began the tradition of having all the Sandringham clocks set half an hour fast. Alongside his numerous hobbies including sailing, bridge, horseracing, and the theatre, Edward was also a keen hunter, who loved to host shooting parties at Sandringham. Thus, to fit in more hours of the day for hunting, especially in the winter when there is less daylight, he established a rule that the clocks should always run half an hour fast, presumably so that his guests would get up a little earlier in the morning than they intended. Edward also kept a set of jockey's weighing scales inside the front door, to check that departing guests had been sufficiently well-fed to have put on a few pounds during their stay.

The tradition of 'Sandringham Time' was maintained by Edward's son, George V, who was also a keen hunter. George loved Sandringham as much as his father had, describing it as, 'Dear old Sandringham, the place I love better than anywhere else in the world.' However, when George's son Edward took the throne in 1936, to become King Edward VIII, he brought the clocks back in line with the rest of the world, and this quirk of royal history came to an end.

Why did Germany scuttle her entire navy?

World War One ended on 11 November 1918, when the defeated German nation signed the Armistice with the Allies. Article XXIII of the Armistice required Germany to hand over her entire navy, to be interned at Scapa Flow, a large natural harbour near Orkney, formed by a ring of Scottish islands. By 25 November, the entire German force of 74 war-ships and more than 200 U-Boats had arrived at Scapa Flow, having lost only one torpedo boat en route, which had struck a mine.

However, there was still a decision to be made about what to do with this enormous fleet. France and Italy wanted the ships to be divided among the Allies, but Britain was not keen, being the dominant naval power of the time, as any split would reduce Britain's relative naval strength. As negotiations for the Treaty of Versailles dragged on, conditions on board the ships deteriorated. Unlike British sailors, the Germans did not tend to spend long periods living on board, and so their quarters did not offer much comfort. A skeleton crew of around 4,800 Germans remained on board the fleet, but there were fears that the sailors were demoralised, ill disciplined, and on the brink of mutiny. Conditions on board were soon said to constitute 'indescribable filth'.

The German commander was Rear-Admiral Ludwig von Reuter, and as the Treaty of Versailles drew nearer to being signed, he began circulating plans among the officers to scuttle the fleet, not wanting the ships to fall into British hands. Britain had anticipated this risk, but were unable to prevent preparations being made, as portholes were loosened, and holes were bored through bulkheads. At 10 am on the morning of 21 June 1919, most of the British battleships left for exercises, and Reuter signalled the German fleet 'Paragraph eleven. Confirm.', which was the code for the fleet to be immediately scuttled. The sailors opened portholes and doors, smashed the internal plumbing, and opened flood valves and seacocks.

Once they realised what was happening, the British First Battle Squadron rushed back to Scapa Flow, but by the time of their return at 2.30pm only the large ships were left afloat. As the British forces tried to prevent the destruction of the fleet, nine Germans were shot and killed, and about sixteen wounded on board their ships. In the end, 52 of the 74 German ships were sunk, with the remainder either remaining afloat, or being towed to shallower waters and beached.

A total of 400,000 tons of modern warships were sunk, which is the largest loss of shipping that has ever taken place on a single day. The Germans were declared to be prisoners-of-war, and heavily criticised by the British for breaching both the Armistice and 'the honourable traditions of seamen of all nations'. However, Britain's leaders were privately thought to be relieved, as the scuttling was actually quite a good outcome, as it resolved the tricky question of redistributing the German fleet, and Britain's naval supremacy was secured. Given that this was Britain's attitude, it's hard not to see the loss of 9 German lives during the scuttling, who turned out to be the last casualties of the First World War, as even more regrettable and futile.

Most of the sunken ships were left at the bottom of the Scapa Flow, as it was not thought worthwhile to try and salvage them, with there already being a glut of scrap metal on the market after the war. However, in 1923 an entrepreneur named Ernest Cox paid £250 to the Admiralty to buy 26 of the sunken destroyers, and then began operations to raise them and salvage them. Cox had developed an innovative new technique, whereby the ships' hulls would be repaired underwater by skilled divers, and then pumped with air, causing the ships to refloat to the surface. Using this technique, Cox managed to salvage 26 destroyers, five battleships, and two battlecruisers. Cox's operation could not even be halted by a coal strike in 1926 – he simply dug out the coal from the submerged *Seydlitz*, brought it to the surface, and then used this coal to power his equipment until the end of the strike.

A number of the wrecks lie in deeper waters, and have never been raised. They now form a popular site for divers. They are also occasionally used to salvage small pieces of steel, to be used in the manufacture of radiation-sensing scientific devices such as Geiger counters. This submerged steel is a precious resource because it was produced before the Second World War, and is thus one of the world's only sources of steel which is free from the possibility of nuclear contamination.

What effect did Prohibition have on American drinking habits?

In 1920, the US government passed the Volstead Act banning the manufacture and sale of alcohol. Because this act required an amendment to the US Constitution (the Eighteenth), it was felt that it would never be repealed, and so Americans believed that they might never again drink freely. Prohibition was not an entirely new phenomenon in the US, as there had been temperance movements since the 18th century, 24 states already had some kind of anti-drink laws, and many states had 'dry' counties, but the Volstead Act made alcohol illegal nationwide, and consequently had a dramatic effect.

So did Prohibition manage to force Americans to step away from the bottle? Statistics are somewhat shaky for this period, because of course the production and selling of alcohol became underground, criminal activities, but all the evidence seems to suggest that rather than declining, American drinking rocketed over the period of Prohibition, which lasted until the act was repealed by the Twenty-First Amendment in 1933. By 1927, drink driving cases in Chicago had risen by 476 per cent compared with the period before Prohibition, and deaths from alcoholism had soared by 600 per cent.

It seems that, rather than dissuading people from drinking, Prohibition made people angry and rebellious, feeling that a civil right had been taken away from them, and alcohol came to take on a disproportionately important place in the national psyche. Illegal bars known as 'speakeasies' opened up throughout major cities, with 30,000 in New York alone. Huge numbers of people took up home distilling, making gin in their bathtubs, or wine made from bizarre fruits and vegetables. Retailers sold bricks of dried grape juice, along with detailed warnings about what steps not to take, to ensure that this grape juice would not accidentally ferment and turn into wine. God forbid.

Before Prohibition, organised crime had been a relatively small phenomenon, dealing chiefly in prostitution and gambling. Now that drinking was illegal, there was an enormous new black market, leading to the rise of a new breed of violent, armed mobsters, including a Chicago gangster named Al Capone. To enforce Prohibition, the authorities had to employ huge numbers of agents at enormous cost. Total sales of alcohol before Prohibition had been around $2 billion a year, but soon the US Treasury Department was spending $2.5 billion on employing 3,000 agents to police the ban. And gangsters like Capone were now in charge of a $4 billion industry, which meant that politicians and police departments could usually be bought, undermining the general rule of law. Ten per cent of Federal agents were sacked for being corrupt, and in many states the police felt it was pointless trying to prosecute bootleggers, as corrupt judges and politicians would never allow a case to stick.

As well as a decline in lawfulness, Prohibition also had a seriously damaging effect on public health. People began distilling alcohol from a whole range of legal products, including perfume, hair tonic, paint, and anti-freeze, with huge numbers of people being poisoned in the process. During one four-day period in 1928, an astonishing 34 people died in New York alone from distilling alcohol. Over the thirteen 'dry' years, 35,000 Americans died from poisonous alcohol.

The last straw was the St Valentine's Day Massacre in 1929, when Al Capone gunned down seven members of the rival O'Banion gang in a Chicago garage. However damaging alcohol had been to pre-Prohibition society, it couldn't have been worse than the violence, crime, and corruption that followed. In the 1932 election, President Hoover campaigned on a strict pro-Prohibition platform, while his Democrat opponent Franklin D. Roosevelt offered America 'a New Deal, and a pot of beer for everyone'. Roosevelt won by a landslide, with 57.4% of the vote against Hoover's 39.7%, and within nine days of his inauguration, Prohibition had been repealed.

What was unusual about Romania's Colonel Corbu?

Colonel Corbu was somewhat unusual for a Romanian army officer, in that he was a dog, a black Labrador to be precise. Corbu, whose name means 'raven' in Romanian, had been given to the Romanian dictator Nicolai Ceauşescu by the British Liberal politician David Steel. Ceauşescu loved the dog, soon elevating it to the rank of colonel in the army. Colonel Corbu was given his own limousine and motorcade, in which he would parade around the center of Bucharest. The British Ambassador described the sight, 'I saw this black dog sitting all on its own in the back of a Dacia, looking rather pompous with its nose in the air, as black Labradors often do.' No one was allowed to feed Colonel Corbu, except for a special doctor, who would check his food first. Of course, Corbu's food would have to be only the very best cuts of meat, as well as Winalot and dog biscuits imported from Britain by the Romanian Ambassador.

On one occasion, Colonel Corbu accompanied President Ceauşescu on a visit to the Brancovenesc Hospital in the centre of Bucharest. The hospital was infested with rats, and so the hospital kept a number of cats, to try and deal with the problem. When Corbu saw one of these cats, he naturally gave chase, being a dog, and a fight ensued. Neither party was badly injured, but Corbu's nose was bloodied, and the hospital staff rightly feared that Ceauşescu would not let such an affront go unpunished; after all, Corbu was a colonel in the President's army. As a result of this incident the hospital, which had treated around 50,000 Romanians the previous year, was closed and demolished.

However, the most disastrous episode of Ceauşescu's reign was his plan to increase Romania's population, by simply banning divorce, abortion, and birth control. Women were regularly inspected by gynaecologists, to ensure they were not using any form of birth control, with extra benefits being offered to women who had 5 and 10 children respectively. Within a year, the birth rate had doubled, but no plans had been made to increase maternity facilities, and infant mortality soared. We still don't know the extent of this disaster, as Ceauşescu brought in a new rule that birth certificates should only be issued once a baby was a month old. As a result, any babies that died before reaching one month simply went unrecorded. The combination of food shortages and a rising birth rate soon meant that hospitals, asylums, and orphanages were filled with unwanted and disabled children, living in dreadful squalor. The situation was made even worse by an epidemic of AIDS among the children, which was caused by an ill-considered plan to give newborn babies blood transfusions, which became contaminated with HIV. In December 1989, after months of crippling food shortages, the Ceauşescus were overthrown in a violent revolution, and executed on Christmas Day, but their consequences of their disastrous regime are still felt today, as Romania still has more orphans than any other European country.

9

PUBLIC IMAGES

'I would much rather have men ask why
I have no statue than why I have one.'
Cato the Elder (234-149 BC)

How was the Emperor Augustus insulted by a bird?

One of Rome's most celebrated leaders was the Emperor Augustus, the heir to Julius Caesar, who ruled from 27-14 BC. Augustus converted Rome from a republic into effectively a hereditary monarchy, known as the principate. This might sound like the first move of a tyrant, but in fact Augustus was far less dictatorial than many of his republican predecessors, and he was widely loved by the people for delivering peace and stability, and expanding the Roman Empire. Augustus was also celebrated for his wit and wisdom, and many examples of this were recorded by the chronicler Ambrosius Theodosius Macrobius, although many of these stories should probably be taken with a pinch of salt, as Macrobius was writing more than 400 years after Augustus's death.

One famous example concerns Augustus's triumphant return to Rome, having defeated Antony and Cleopatra at the Battle of Actium. This was a decisive victory, which ended the Roman Civil War, and avenged the death of Augustus's great-uncle Julius Caesar. On his triumphant journey home, Augustus was greeted by a man with a raven, which had been taught to say, 'Greetings to Caesar, our victorious commander!'. ('Caesar' was Augustus's adoptive surname, which came to be synonymous with the word 'Emperor', later becoming corrupted as the German 'Kaiser' and Russian 'Tsar'). Augustus was impressed by the talented bird, and moved by the man's obvious loyalty, as it would have taken many months to train the raven, and the outcome of the Civil War had been by no means certain. As a reward, Augustus paid the man the enormous sum of twenty thousand sesterces for the bird.

However, it turned out that the bird trainer had a business partner, but failed to share any of this good fortune with him. The partner was angry, so he approached Augustus, and told him that the bird trainer had a second raven, which Augustus might also like to inspect. Augustus summoned the bird, which repeated a phrase of its own, in this case, 'Greetings to Antony, our victorious commander!' Luckily for the resourceful bird trainer, Augustus was amused rather than angered by the duplicitous scheme, and punished the man only by ordering him to share the money with his partner.

Augustus's easy-going nature is also evident in that he seems to have even allowed stories to be circulated in which he was the butt of the joke. On one occasion, again described by Macrobius, Augustus had heard stories about a man from the provinces, who was said to look eerily like Augustus himself. The Emperor summoned the man, and once he saw him, he couldn't help but agree: the resemblance was uncanny. 'Tell me, young man,' the Emperor asked, 'was your mother ever in Rome?'. 'No,' the young man cheekily replied, 'but my father was; often.'

How was the coronation of William the Conqueror interrupted?

The reign of William the Conqueror was famously cruel and brutal. In Normandy, he had been known by the nickname William the Bastard, and while this had been a reference to his illegitimate birth, rather than his character, many in England might have felt it was particularly apt. After winning the Battle of Hastings, William quickly defeated the south of England, but resistance in the north would continue for another six years, with support from Scotland, Northumbria, and the Vikings. William eventually won victory through a savage scorched earth policy known as the 'Harrying of the North', in which his men were ordered to set fire to every house, every crop, and even the people's tools. As a result, northern England was left barren and scarred, and it was said that there was 'left no house standing and no man alive that could be found' between the Humber and the Tyne. A dreadful famine followed, and it took many generations for the land to recover.

William's coronation reflected both his unpopularity and his ruthlessness. As the ceremony took place at Westminster Abbey, William's guards were disturbed by noises nearby, so they set fire to the neighbouring houses. The fires quickly spread, causing chaos inside and outside the Abbey, and people variously panicked, tried to fight the fire, or simply took the opportunity to indulge in a spot of looting.

William generally had bad luck with it came to the dignity of ceremonial events. Even after his death, his funeral was interrupted by an angry local man named Asselin, who insisted that the land upon which William was to be buried had previously been stolen from him, by William himself. In what must have been an embarrassing scene, the man was quickly paid off by William's son Henry, with what was considered a fair price for the land.

Even then, the unpleasantness was not yet over, as William's body could not be squeezed into the stone sarcophagus which had been chosen for it. Although he had been very fit as a young man, William had become extremely fat towards the end of his life, and his corpse had swollen between his death and the funeral, as a result of the warm weather and the time that had passed. The bishops were forced to suffer the indignity of trying to cram William's bloated body into the coffin, but as they tried to force it down, the corpse's stomach burst, and rotting flesh spewed out, 'filling the church with a foul smell.'

Why did Henry II submit to being whipped by monks in 1174?

The whipping of King Henry II was the strange eventual outcome of the breakdown in the king's relationship with his former friend Thomas Becket, whose name is sometimes written as Thomas à Becket. Becket was born in London to middle-class parents in 1118. An intelligent and diligent child, he was soon taken under the wing of a wealthy family friend, Richer de L'Aigle, who taught him gentlemanly pursuits, such as horse riding, jousting, and hunting. From the age of ten, Becket received a first-class education, travelling to some of the leading cities in Europe, and when he returned to England, he attracted the attention of Theobald, the Archbishop of Canterbury, who quickly promoted the young Becket to a senior position in the clergy.

When the office of Lord Chancellor became vacant, Theobald recommended Becket to King Henry II. The two soon
became firm friends, as Becket helped Henry to pursue his
domestic agenda, which chiefly consisted of Henry's desire to
levy taxes on the Church and remove the clergy's traditional
privileges. Becket carried out his duties with his usual zeal, and
quickly earned the enmity of many in the Church, particularly
given the extravagant, courtly life he was seen to be enjoying.
Henry and Becket were so close that the King even sent his
son, also called Henry, to live with Becket, in a form of foster-
ing which was not uncommon among the nobility of the time.

In 1162, Theobald died, and Henry appointed Becket as
the new Archbishop of Canterbury, marking an astonishing rise. As you might expect, Henry was confident that the
appointment of his friend would make his relationship with
the Church much smoother. However, Becket's career so far
had been characterised not so much by loyalty, but rather by
diligence and application, and he now seems to have taken the
same approach to his new role, becoming a staunch defender
of the Church, and blocking Henry's reforms at every step.
The sticking point was the issue of ecclesiastical courts. Henry
wanted clergymen who were charged with serious crimes
such as murder to be tried in secular courts, rather than the
church courts, but Becket refused. This was an issue of some
significance, as at this time around one sixth of England's
population were considered to be clergymen, and there had
been many examples of dreadful crimes being lightly treated
by the ecclesiastical courts. The conflict came to a head at
the assemblies of Clarendon Palace in 1164, at which Becket
refused to ratify the King's sixteen 'constitutions' (these were
new laws curbing the Church's power). Having reached this

impasse, the two men were now effectively at war, and Becket was forced to flee to the Continent.

By 1170, Henry was on the point of allowing Becket to return, as he was under considerable pressure from the Pope and clergy. However, in June of that year the conflict escalated again, sparked by the coronation of Henry the Young King in York. This event will need a little explaining, as King Henry II was still very much alive, but there was a French tradition of crowning the young heir apparent during the current monarch's lifetime, to avoid succession disputes; and Henry himself was of course French. So when, in June 1170, Henry II had his son Henry crowned, there were now effectively two kings, although Henry the Young King was clearly understood to be the junior of the two.

The coronation of Henry the Young King infuriated Becket, because traditionally the privilege of crowning a monarch had belonged to Canterbury, and so Becket was outraged at this snub to the prestige of his office, as he was still Archbishop of Canterbury. In retaliation, he began issuing a series of excommunications, starting with the Archbishop of York and the bishops of London and Salisbury, who had carried out the coronation.

Henry was in Normandy, and sick in bed, when he heard the news of Becket's actions, and he exclaimed in frustration, 'Will no one rid me of this turbulent priest?'. Or at least, those are the words he is usually reported to have said. A contemporary Latin source records that what Henry actually said was, 'What miserable drones and traitors have I nourished and brought up in my household, who let their lord be treated with such shameful contempt by a low-born cleric?'. The distinction is important, because the first version is clearly closer to being an instruction, whereas the second sounds like a complaint, but not an order. We may not know exactly what was said, but we do know that those present took Henry's words to be a royal command, and made plans to deal with the king's nemesis. Four knights now travelled to Canterbury, and attempted to arrest Becket. When he refused to come, they drew their swords and cut him down in the main hall of the cathedral, with one blow cutting off the crown of his head, as blood stained the cathedral floor.

After the murder, Henry claimed that he had never intended to give the order, and it seems plausible that this was true. After all, if he had really intended to order Becket's murder, why would he do it in front of so many witnesses, in such an oblique way, rather than simply arranging it privately and explicitly? Henry also showed a remarkable willingness to observe penance, which also suggests that this was a genuine misunderstanding, although he was also under considerable political pressure. Killing an archbishop inside a cathedral was a serious matter, and the Pope was threatening to excommunicate Henry. Furthermore, England was on the brink of war with both Scotland and a Flemish armada.

To appease the Pope, Henry agreed to a number of penances, including restoring rights to the clergy and the archbishopric of Canterbury. He also agreed to travel to Canterbury personally, and to walk through the stony streets barefoot. By the time he reached the cathedral, his feet were sore and bloody. There, he allowed the monks to whip him repeatedly, to atone for his sins. For years afterwards, Henry expressed genuine regret about the death of his former friend.

Why is Richard the Lionheart so revered?

Henry's son Richard the Lionheart is one of England's most venerated kings, and one of the few who are remembered by their honorific, rather than simply their number. A heroic statue of Richard stands outside the House of Parliament, while the well established legend of Robin Hood includes a portrayal of Richard as a noble, just, and merciful Crusader, whose reign was blighted by the actions of his weak, greedy brother, John.

However, it's not clear how Richard has gained such a celebrated reputation, as the facts of his reign are somewhat different from the legend. Far from being an English hero, Richard was French. He was born in 1157 to French parents, and spoke only French, and no English. He lived in France for most of his life, and had no interest in England, which he treated simply as a bottomless purse with which to fund his wars. Over the course of his ten-year reign from 1189-1199, he spent fewer than six months in England, and no time at all during the last five years. Over this period, he emptied the treasury to fund his Crusading, and sold off as many lands, titles, and jobs as he could. He effectively sold Scotland for 10,000 marks, and declared, 'I would have sold London if I could find a buyer.' He also used England to supply his army with men, and many thousands lost their lives on Richard's failed Third Crusade. After the Crusade, Richard was kidnapped, and only returned to England after an enormous ransom of 150,000 marks had been paid. This monumental sum was around three times the annual income of the Crown, and could only be raised by the levying of enormous one-off taxes, which caused considerable hardship in England.

A key part of Richard's legend is founded on his military prowess, and it does seem that he was a successful warrior and tactician. However, his Third Crusade was an expensive failure, as he failed to recapture Jerusalem, and was forced to enter into a truce with Saladin in 1192. Richard was renowned as much for his brutality as for his tactical acumen. His French subjects frequently rebelled against his cruelty, which included accusations of rape, and the execution of prisoners of war. During the Third Crusade, Richard had nearly 2,700 Muslim hostages executed, when sufficient ransom wasn't paid. Richard's treatment of Jews was notably barbaric; after his accession to the English throne, Jewish leaders who had come to pay their respects were stripped and flogged, and there was a London-wide massacre, which was believed to have been ordered by Richard. According to a well established legend, members of Richard's House of Anjou dynasty were believed to have the devil's blood running in their veins, and Richard encouraged this belief.

Richard is sometimes portrayed as being honest and just, in contrast to his slippery, deceiving brother John, but in fact Richard was arguably even more treacherous than his brother. In 1173 Richard and his brothers attempted to overthrow their father, Henry II, perhaps at the instigation of their mother, Eleanor of Aquitaine (the bare-breasted Crusader). When the plot failed, Richard begged his father for forgiveness, crying at his feet. Henry forgave his son, but ten years later Richard challenged Henry again, and the ensuing war is thought to have led to Henry's death.

One aspect of Richard's life which is rarely mentioned is that he was almost certainly gay. His public confessions and penitences appear to have acknowledged the sin of sodomy. He married Berengaria of Navarre in 1191, but the pair spent hardly any time together before separating, and it's not clear whether the marriage was even consummated. He may possibly have fathered one illegitimate son, but he produced no other children, and this failure to provide an heir caused considerable instability after Richard's death, effectively leading to the break-up of the Angevin Empire. His friendship with King Philip II of France is said to have been so close that they ate from the same plate, and slept in the same bed. Some historians claim that this was merely a political gesture, with no sexual connotations, but it is up to the reader to judge whether not this explanation is credible.

So does this mean that King John was misjudged too?

If Richard the Lionheart was not quite the heroic figure of legend, does this mean that his brother King John ought also to be reevaluated? Well, John does seem to have been somewhat maligned by history. According to some historians he was an efficient administrator, who was hindered by a series of ongoing attacks from the barons and other enemies. John ordered a massive expansion in England's shipbuilding, and in the process arguably laid the foundations for the modern Royal Navy.

However, despite his arguable merits, King John does deserve many of the criticisms which are laid at his door. His reputation for treachery is well deserved – he was involved in the campaign to oust his father Henry II, and also conspired against his brother Richard over Aquitaine. He imprisoned his niece Eleanor, Fair Maid of Brittany until her death in 1241, and he may have killed his nephew Arthur by his own hand. Later, when Richard was kidnapped by the Duke of Austria after the Third Crusade, John offered to pay the Duke not for Richard's release, but to keep him imprisoned, so that John could steal the throne. However, the plot failed, as their mother Eleanor of Aquitaine managed to raise the ransom, but had to pawn the Crown Jewels to do so.

His military record was disastrous, earning him the nicknames John Softsword and John Lackland. Over the course of his reign, John lost all of England's lands in France, and these costly failures did lead to some rather sneaky tax rises, including England's first income tax, even if the economy had already been crippled by Richard's wars and ransom. John spent much of his reign in conflict with the barons and the Pope, and came off worse in both cases. In 1213, John was forced to surrender all religious authority in England to the Pope. In 1215, the barons forced John to sign the Magna Carta, severely curtailing the power of the Crown.

John's endless conflict with the barons seems to have stemmed at least in part from his lecherous behaviour, which included habitually trying to sleep with their wives and daughters. On one occasion, he made clear his intention to seduce Margaret, the wife of Eustace de Vesci. Knowing that John would come to Margaret's room that night, de Vesci substituted a prostitute in her place. The next morning, John brazenly boasted to Eustace about how good his wife had been in bed, so Eustace told him how he had been deceived, before quickly escaping.

King John's final days provided a fitting end to his calamitous reign. Having signed the Magna Carta, he then attempted to renege on it, leading to the First Barons' War, and a French invasion by Prince Louis. By the summer of 1216, John had lost Northern England to the Scots, and much of the South to Louis. Isolated in Lincolnshire, and suffering from dysentery, John attempted to take a shortcut across a stretch of water in the Wash, but the tide rose quickly, and his baggage train became submerged, losing all of his treasures, including the Crown Jewels. A few days later John died, to be succeeded by his nine year old son, Henry III.

Which queen gave birth before an audience of 200 people?

After the death of Charles II in 1685, the crown of England passed to his brother James, who would rule as James II in England and Ireland, and James VII in Scotland. Although James was a Catholic, the public were said to be pleased at the orderly succession, and Parliament was also supportive, granting James a healthy income. Even when James's rule proved to be as pro-Catholic as many had feared, England's Protestants were generally tolerant, safe in the knowledge that James's wife Mary of Modena seemed to be unable to produce an heir, which meant that the crown would pass to one of his two daughters from his first marriage, Mary and Anne, who were both Protestants. England's period of Catholic rule was therefore likely to be short, and thus tolerable.

However, after ten unsuccessful pregnancies, Mary of Modena did manage to produce a male heir, when in 1688 she gave birth to James Francis Edward. Because of the rumour and innuendo that had dogged previous successions, the birthing room was filled with witnesses – the number has been estimated at anywhere between 67 and 200, with the Lord Chancellor watching proceedings closely at the end of the bed. This audience included a mixture of Protestants and Catholics, in the hope of ensuring that no side could dispute the child's legitimacy, but there are reports that the Protestants present simply turned their back on the scene, refusing to bear witness.

As a result, and despite the great number of witnesses present, rumours immediately began to spread that the child had in fact been stillborn, and that the baby now being displayed as the apparent prince had in fact been smuggled into the birthing room in a warming pan. As the controversy grew,

James and Mary of Modena were forced to flee to France, and Parliament offered the crown to the Dutch prince William of Orange (as previously described in Chapter Two).

A similar scene of crowded childbirth is said to have almost killed France's Marie Antoinette in 1778. There was considerable excitement when the time came to give birth, as although the young Queen was only 23, she had been married to King Louis XVI for eight years without producing a child. The protocol for a royal birth was that spectators would only enter the birthing room at the moment of delivery, but such was the excitement that when the announcement was made, the crowd of spectators surged into the room, and would have crushed the young Queen had the bed not been ringed with tapestry screens. As the room filled, and people starting climbing onto furniture, the Queen fainted, apparently suffocated by the heat of the room, and the lack of oxygen. The windows of the birthing room had been sealed shut, but luckily Louis was an unusually tall and powerful man, and he managed to force one open, and the Queen was revived. After this incident, the tradition was ended at Marie Antoinette's insistence, and only a select handful of relatives and ministers would attend the queen's future births.

When was Britain's Royal Navy used to protect the drugs trade?

As amazing as it may sound, in the 19th century Britain went to war twice to protect Britain's growing trade in opium, and used the Royal Navy to defend the rights of illegal drug smugglers. Opium was the key issue in two wars between Britain and China which became known as the Opium Wars, between 1839-42 and 1856-60.

The background to the crisis was China's traditional resistance to trade of any kind, as Confucian philosophy held the view that trade would lead to unrest and conflict. In the late 17th century, China's ruling Qing dynasty demonstrated its hostility to maritime trade when it issued a decree evacuating the entire coastal population of Southern China, a ban which lasted from 1661 to 1669.

China did engage in some trade with the European powers from around the 16th century onwards, but it only took place under certain strict conditions. Foreign diplomats and governments were only allowed to engage with China under the tributary system, which meant that they were required to pay tribute to the Emperor, recognising the superiority of the imperial court, and the Emperor's mandate to rule on Earth as God's appointed representative. In return, dignitaries might receive lavish gifts, which served to display China's supremacy and wealth, as well as perhaps the rights to lucrative, short-term trade.

From the 1630s onwards, European companies were also permitted to trade at a number of Chinese ports, outside of the tributary system, but this trade was subject to import duties as high as 20 percent. A further restriction was that the Chinese would only accept silver as payment, which meant that there was an increasing drain of silver away from Europe, and into China, over the 17th century. This was a particular problem for Britain, which had adopted the gold standard, and had therefore to buy silver from European rivals such as Spain, adding an additional cost to this trading relationship.

What was needed was a product which China was keen to buy from Britain – that way, the trade deficit would be reduced. In the 18th century, Britain found the perfect product: opium. Having annexed Bengal in 1757, Britain now had a monopoly on India's opium. Opium as a product had obvious and proven consumer appeal, and was highly addictive. It also happened to be illegal in China, but Britain's approach was to treat this prohibition as a commercial opportunity, rather than an ethical or diplomatic issue. Through the state-owned East India Company, Britain began importing opium into China, in enormous chests which held 140 pounds each, using Chinese smugglers to minimise the appearance of British involvement. Despite China's repeated protests and decrees against Britain's disregard for Chinese law, the opium trade soared, and Britain went from importing 15 tons of opium into China in 1730, to 900 tons a year by the 1820s.

By 1839 the trade had grown to more than 1,400 tons per year, and China's patience was at an end. Native drug smugglers were sentenced to death, and British traders were imprisoned in their factories and denied food. Chinese troops boarded British ships and destroyed the opium on board, by dissolving it with salt, water, and lime, and then throwing it overboard. The Chinese commissioner wrote to Queen Victoria, insisting on China's determination to rid itself of this harmful drug, and questioning the morality of Britain's behaviour in engaging in this trade. Britain's response was to send the Royal Navy, whose superior warships and artillery soon won a dramatic victory, devastating China's coastal economy.

By 1842, China was ready to surrender, and so the Treaty of Nanjing was signed. This was the first of what became known as the Unequal Treaties, a series of agreements which were perceived as undermining Chinese sovereignty, and were considered a national embarrassment. The Treaty of Nanjing required China to hand over Hong Kong to Britain, as well as paying a huge indemnity for the destroyed opium, and opening up four ports to trade. There would be further treaties with Britain over the following decades, as well as with France and the United States, as each nation insisted of being granted the same rights as her rivals. There was also a Second Opium War, between 1856-1860, after China attempted to resist British trade.

Britain may have won the Opium Wars, but the conflict nonetheless left a bad taste in many people's mouths. In the House of Commons, a young MP named William Gladstone responded to the First Opium War in 1841 by stating that if there had ever been, 'a war more unjust in its origin, a war more calculated to cover this country with permanent disgrace, I do not know.' Many feel that the humiliation suffered by China during the Opium Wars, when it was effectively forced to become a semi-colonial possession, is still keenly felt today, affecting China's current relations with Western powers.

Which leader held a state funeral for his own leg?

The answer is Mexico's former president Antonio de Santa Anna, who was one of the most extraordinary figures in American history. He was born in the state of Vera Cruz in 1794, and joined the army as a cadet at the age of 16. He fought initially for the Spanish against Mexican independence, but switched sides in 1821, helping to bring about an independent Mexico, with Augustin de Iturbide as Head of State. Throughout his career, Santa Anna would switch sides whenever it suited him, apparently being motivated only by a desire to make sure he ended up on the winning side. In 1828, his support was enough to hand the presidency to the candidate who had lost the election, and as a reward Santa Anna was made the highest-ranking general in the land.

However, Santa Anna's ambitions were far from being fulfilled, and by 1833 he had installed himself as President of Mexico. Over the next 22 years, Santa Anna would hold the presidency on an astonishing eleven separate, non-consecutive occasions. No matter how many times he was ousted or defeated, he always seemed to find a way to manoeuvre himself back into power, aided by his importance as a military leader. When Texas declared independence from Mexico in 1835, Santa Anna led the counter-attack at the famous Battle of the Alamo, and ordered the policy of executing all prisoners, in what became known as the Goliad Massacre. Santa Anna's army was soon defeated at the decisive Battle of San Jacinto, where the Texan revolutionaries were inspired by the battle cry, 'Remember Goliad! Remember the Alamo!'.

Over the course of his reign, Santa Anna increasingly turned the presidency into a personality cult, with himself at the centre, described variously as 'The Napoleon of the West', 'The Victor of Tampico', and 'The Savior of the Motherland'. In 1838, Santa Anna displayed remarkable courage in defeating a French invasion force at Vera Cruz, having a number of horses shot from beneath him in the course of the fighting. As a result of his injuries, his left leg had to be amputated below the knee.

This led to one of the most extraordinary incidents in Santa Anna's bizarre career. At first, he kept the leg at his hacienda, for four years. He then decided that it deserved a more prominent place in public life, and so paraded it around the streets of Mexico on September 26, 1842, accompanied by bands and orchestras, before laying it to rest in a national shrine known as the Pantheon of Saint Paula.

After losing his leg, Santa Anna wore a prosthetic leg made of cork. During the Mexican-American War of 1846-8, this leg was captured by American troops, and it is now displayed in the Illinois State Military Museum in Springfield. The Mexican government has asked for it to be returned on a number of occasions, but so far the museum has refused, stating, 'It's an important part of Illinois history.'

Which 272-word speech was described the following day by the Chicago Times as 'silly', 'flat', and 'dishwatery'?

The answer is the Gettysburg Address, which is now of course regarded as one of the most powerful speeches of American history. A recent article in Time magazine deemed it to be one of the ten greatest speeches ever made. The speech was delivered by President Abraham Lincoln in 1863, on the occasion of the consecration of the Soldiers' National Cemetery at Gettysburg, Pennsylvania. Only four months earlier, the Union forces had won a decisive victory at Gettysburg, halting the northwards advance of Robert E. Lee's Confederate army. Gettysburg would turn out to be the biggest battle of the Civil War, leaving a battlefield strewn with the bodies of more than 7,500 soldiers and 5,000 horses, decomposing in the hot July air.

In response, the residents of Gettysburg arranged for a national cemetery to be built, and invited President Lincoln to deliver a few remarks, which would follow the official speech, to be delivered by the former senator Edward Everett. Everett's two-hour oration has since been largely forgotten, but Lincoln's brief remarks which followed have continued to ring out. In just two minutes, Lincoln offered a vision of unity for the nation, as well as restating the moral purpose of the war, to create a democratic society of equals:

Four score and seven years ago our fathers brought forth on this continent a new nation, conceived in liberty, and dedicated to the proposition that all men are created equal.

Now we are engaged in a great civil war, testing whether that nation, or any nation, so conceived and so dedicated, can long endure. We are met on a great battle-field of that war. We have come to dedicate a portion of that field, as a final resting place for those who here gave their lives that that nation might live. It is altogether fitting and proper that we should do this.

But, in a larger sense, we can not dedicate, we can not consecrate, we can not hallow this ground. The brave men, living and dead, who struggled here, have consecrated it, far above our poor power to add or detract. The world will little note, nor long remember what we say here, but it can never forget what they did here. It is for us the living, rather, to be dedicated here to the unfinished work which they who fought here have thus far so nobly advanced. It is rather for us to be here dedicated to the great task remaining before us —that from these honored dead we take increased devotion to that cause for which they gave the last full measure of devotion—that we here highly resolve that these dead shall not have died in vain — that this nation, under God, shall have a new birth of freedom — and that government of the people, by the people, for the people, shall not perish from the earth.

It was a powerful and inspiring speech, and yet not everyone was moved. According to some accounts, the speech was met with silence, or sparse applause which was 'barely polite', perhaps because many felt the speech 'seemed short'. Lincoln himself reportedly felt it had gone badly, describing it as 'a flat failure'. The following day, the – admittedly partisan,

Democrat-supporting - Chicago Times commented, 'The cheek of every American must tingle with shame as he reads the silly, flat and dishwatery utterances of the man who has to be pointed out to intelligent foreigners as the President of the United States.'

How did a US President inspire one the world's best-loved toys?

The president in question was Theodore Roosevelt, who is widely considered to be have been one of America's greatest presidents and statesmen. He was sworn in to the White House in 1901, after President McKinley was assassinated, becoming the youngest president in US history at just 42. Roosevelt's many achievements as president included the completion of the Panama Canal, negotiating the end of the Russo-Japanese war (for which he was awarded the Nobel Peace Prize, making him the first American to win a Nobel Prize of any kind), and a domestic agenda based on what he called a 'Square Deal', which meant a growth in antitrust and business regulations, and improvements in consumer rights.

In 1902, President Roosevelt travelled to the South, to deal with a border dispute between Louisiana and Mississippi. He was a keen hunter, and so while he was there, his hosts arranged a bear hunting trip. On the day, the organisers were anxious to provide a bear for the President to shoot, but the only specimen they could find was a wounded young black bear, which they clubbed and tied to a willow tree, before inviting Roosevelt to shoot it. The President declined, feeling that there wasn't much sport in killing such a weakened and defenceless animal. However, because the bear was clearly in pain, he ordered it to be put down as a mercy killing, to put it out of its misery.

This incident became the subject of a famous cartoon by Clifford K. Berryman, called 'Drawing the Line in Mississippi', which attempted to draw a satirical link between the Louisiana-Mississippi border dispute and Roosevelt's treatment of the bear. However, the cute bear drawn by Berryman in the cartoon became associated with Roosevelt, and soon a Brooklyn candy-store owner named Morris Michtom approached the President to ask if he could use his name for a new toy that he had invented, which was a cute stuffed bear, inspired by the cartoon. Roosevelt agreed, and so Michtom began producing 'Teddy's Bear', which became a big hit (Teddy of course being the shortened form of the President's first name 'Theodore') . For years, in fact, stuffed bears were known mainly as 'Teddy's Bear' or 'Roosevelt Bear', before the name evolved into the more familiar 'Teddy Bear'.

One of the ironies of this story is that Berryman's cartoon was not really intended to be a cute illustration of the bear story at all. Instead, it was a reference to Mississippi's racially-charged upcoming gubernatorial election, in which the Democratic candidate was a white supremacist called James Vardaman, who supported lynching, and was known as the 'Great White Chief'. Roosevelt was an outspoken critic of Vardaman, and publicly opposed the racist policies of many Southern states. The depiction of an American black bear, with a rope around its neck, being mercifully and protectively treated by the President thus carried a symbolic meaning which seems to have quickly been forgotten, as people simply remembered the association of Roosevelt with the cute cartoon bear.

Who completed an 18-hole round of golf in just 34 shots?

The answer is Kim Jong-Il, North Korea's diminutive

'Supreme Leader'. In doing so, he amazingly managed to outdo the best rounds of golf ever played by professionals, by a staggering margin of 25 shots. Kim's round, which took place at the Pyongyang championship course in October 1994, contained just the five holes-in-one. Most remarkably of all, it was the first time he had ever played the game. After the round, Kim graciously retired from the sport, to give everyone else a chance.

This is just one example of the strange personality cult which exists around Kim Jong-Il, who has been in sole charge of North Korea since his father's death in 1994. North Koreans are besieged by propaganda in praise of Kim, who is known as the Supreme Leader, Dear Leader, Our Father, the General, and the Generalissimo. Pictures of Kim and his father are said to adorn a wall of every home, and on every major road one lane is always kept empty, reserved for the Dear Leader. Other examples of Korean propaganda include the claim that Kim is the world's most revered statesman, as well as being a fighter pilot, an internet expert, and the composer of a number of operas and musicals.

Although the propaganda concerning Kim's life contains some astonishing claims, the facts of his life are only slightly less far fetched. For example, Kim maintains a completely empty, fictional city, which is there just to be seen. Its name is Kijong-Dong, and it is situated in the northern half of the Korean Demilitarized Zone, where it is designed to woo South Koreans to defect to the North. The buildings are brightly painted, and the streetlights go on and off at set times, but no one lives there, it is purely for show. Kijong-Dong also contains the world's largest flagpole, at an astonishing 160 metres high, after an ongoing contest with South Korea in what became known as the 'flagpole war'.

Kim is a film buff, with a collection of 20,000 DVDs. He has written books on the subject, and even produced a number of films himself, after kidnapping South Korean director Shin Sang-ok and his wife. The couple were kept prisoner, and forced to produce a number of films for Kim, including a Godzilla rip-off named 'Pulgasari'. Eventually, when filming for Kim in Austria, they managed to escape from their handlers, and found sanctuary at the US embassy. Kim is believed to be the world's biggest buyer of Hennessy cognac, importing $700,000 worth of the stuff per year, which he drinks in the company of his 'Pleasure Squad' of young concubines. While his people suffer poverty and food shortages, Kim enjoys four-day banquets, feasting on steak, lobster, and Bordeaux wine.

Kim is believed to be 69 years old, and is not expected to live for much longer, as he has suffered a number of strokes, and may be suffering from pancreatic cancer. However, the likelihood seems to be that the leadership of North Korea will pass on to one of his sons, and so the disastrous dynasty may well continue.

10

MENTAL AGES

'History... is a nightmare from which I am trying to awake.'
Ulysses, James Joyce (1882-1941)

What was the source of the Delphic oracle's prophecies?

In all the historical accounts of Ancient Greece, one of the most consistently recorded figures is that of the oracle at Delphi, also know as the Pythia, who could interpret the will of the god Apollo. People of all classes would travel long distances to consult the Pythia and hear her prophecies, which would then determine their actions, anything from when farmers should plant their crops to when armies should go to war. The Greeks, and later the Romans, regularly consulted the oracle for more than a thousand years, from around the 9th century BC, to the 4th century AD. The role of the Pythia would be performed by a priestess, who was required to be pure and of good character. According to one account, the job was traditionally given to young virgins, until one was abducted and raped, after which it was decided that the Pythia should in future be an old woman.

To consult the Pythia, supplicants would go through an elaborate series of rituals, including interviews with the Pythia's priests, animal sacrifices, and gift-giving. Eventually, those who were deemed suitable were shown into a small underground chamber, where the Pythia sat on a three-legged stool, above a crack in the rock. Seemingly in a trance, she would recount her prophecy, although some accounts suggest that this was likely to have been a kind of frenzied speaking-in-tongues; in other words, gibberish. The Pythia's priests would now 'interpret' the prophecy, and provide a more intelligible version, often in the form of verse. Many of these prophecies have been recorded, and although they must have been thought accurate by people of the time, they are often so vague as to be effectively meaningless, a bit like the horoscopes and psychics of today.

The magical powers of the site at Delphi were said to have been discovered by a goatherd named Coretas, who noticed that one of his goats which had fallen into a chasm began behaving strangely. He then climbed into the chasm himself, and found that he was filled with euphoria and divine inspiration, and felt able to foresee the future. As news of this amazing crevice spread, a shrine was erected at the site, which people would visit to experience the intoxicating effects for themselves. After a time, a young woman was chosen to act as the conduit for the divine visions, and she thus came to be seen as the mouthpiece of the gods.

The historian Plutarch worked for a time as a priest at the Delphi site, and he described the Pythia's visions as being caused by vapours, rising from a crack in the chamber floor. It seems that he was correct, as the most likely explanation for the Pythia's trances and strange incantations is that she was breathing in hallucinogenic vapours, which rose from the fissure. In 2001, a team of scientists found that the site of the oracle is exactly on the intersection of two major fault lines, where the bedrock is rich in hydrocarbons. This area is prone to earthquakes, which have the effect of heating this bedrock, vaporising the hydrocarbon chemicals, which then rise to the surface as a gas. One chemical which has been found in the spring waters today is ethylene, which is a powerful hallucinogen, would have exactly the effect described by the Greek historians. Inhaling just a small amount of ethylene can cause euphoria, delirium, trances, and altered speech patterns.

The detail of the contemporary accounts also supports the idea that ethylene may have been the cause of the Pythia's visions. Plutarch described her cavern as having a sweet smell at those times when the supernatural effect was most powerful, and ethylene does indeed have a sweet smell. This may also explain why it was important for the oracle to conduct her prophecies in a small, enclosed chamber, to keep the vapours contained. Before any visitor could see the oracle, they would sacrifice an animal, usually a goat, which would first be washed in the waters of the spring, and then observed to see whether its legs shook. If the goat's legs did not shake in the correct way, this was taken to be a sign that Apollo was not ready to speak, but a more scientific explanation is that this meant that the level of intoxicating ethylene vapour was low that day, and so the oracle would therefore be unable to perform.

After many centuries, the Delphic oracle was felt to have lost its powers, and so the practice died out. One possible explanation for this decline is that there may have been less earthquakes than normal around this time, meaning that less of the hydrocarbons were being vapourised, and so the Pythia would no longer have felt any hallucinogenic effects.

What was unusual about the Roman senator Incitatus?

Incitatus was a horse, and apparently a very special horse, as he was Caligula's favourite. Caligula ruled the Roman Empire from 37-41 AD, and he was famously fond of his four-legged friend. Incitatus lived in a stable made of marble, with an ivory manger. He was dressed in a purple blanket - purple being the colour worn by Roman Emperors and dignitaries - wearing a collar studded with precious jewels. His oats contained flakes of gold, and he was attended by as many as eighteen servants. Incitatus was made a citizen of Rome, and then a senator, and Caligula even had plans to make him a consul, but these were thwarted when the Emperor was assassinated.

Caligula was a famously mad tyrant. He is said to have killed his predecessor (and great uncle) Tiberius, although since Tiberius at this point was 77 and probably dying anyway, this claim may be unreliable. Caligula's accession was initially celebrated by the Roman people, largely because they had hated Tiberius, but Caligula's cruelty, extravagance, and sexual perversity soon destroyed all popular support. Caligula committed incest with at least one of his three sisters, and may have prostituted them to other men (although it should be noted that incest, while unacceptable in Ancient Rome, was less shocking and unusual than it is today). Caligula often boasted of sleeping with other men's wives, and on one occasion kidnapped a woman on her wedding day, married her himself, before divorcing her weeks later, returning her to her former fiancé.

In one bizarre incident, Caligula murdered his adopted son Gemellus, supposedly because he smelled cough syrup on Gemellus's breath. Caligula assumed that the cough syrup was intended as an antidote for poison, which therefore proved that Gemellus feared being poisoned by Caligula. Caligula, insulted at being the object of this implicit suspicion, had the young man killed. In other words Caligula killed him simply for the crime of suspecting that Caligula might kill him. Or, even more absurdly, for the crime of having a bit of a cough. Caligula also killed numerous other family members for spurious reasons, including his father-in-law, brother-in-law, and grandmother. He also forced his former ally Marco to commit suicide.

Although Caligula was clearly a monster, there does seem to have been a small degree of method to his madness. One of his more astonishing acts was to build a floating bridge across the Bay of Baiae, made of a platform of boats covered with earth, across a distance of more than two miles. He then rode Incitatus across this 'bridge', while wearing the breastplate of Alexander the Great. This apparently bizarre act was intended to disprove the prediction of Tiberius's soothsayer Thrasyllus of Mendes that Caligula 'had no more chance of becoming Emperor than of riding a horse across the Bay of Baiae.'

There even seems to have been a kind of logic to his appointment of Incitatus to the Senate. Before Caligula's ascent, the Senate had largely ruled alone, as Tiberius had withdrawn from the city completely, decamping to Capri in 26 AD. Caligula on the other hand decided to take on the power of the Senate, charging a number of senators with treason, and executing those found guilty. In this context, the appointment of Incitatus seems less an act of madness than a deliberate insult to the Senate as a whole, to show Caligula's contempt for the assembly, which he had by this point stripped of any influence or power. However, the Senate seems to have got its own back eventually, as many senators are believed to have been involved when Caligula was assassinated by his own bodyguards, the Praetorian Guard.

Why was King Carlos II of Spain known as Carlos 'The Hexed'?

Carlos II of Spain was plagued by misfortune, to such an extent that many people believed that he had been cursed, a view to which Carlos himself subscribed. 'Many people believe I am bewitched,' he said, 'and I well believe it, such are the things I suffer.' Carlos suffered from a number of physical and mental disabilities from birth. He had a huge, misshapen head, with a jaw that protruded to such an extent that his teeth were some way from being able to meet, and as a result he was unable to chew. His tongue was so large that his speech was almost incoherent. He also suffered from suppurating blisters, diseased bones, and epileptic fits.

Unsurprisingly, Carlos was severely affected by his various ailments. He was unable to speak before the age of four, wet-nursed until around five or six, and only able to walk from the age of eight. Because of his condition, he was not required to receive any kind of education, nor even to maintain what might be considered a basic level of personal hygiene. Instead he was ignored but tolerated, while his mother Mariana of Austria ruled as Regent.

The most likely cause of Carlos's ill health is that he was the result of a long process of inbreeding. For generations, Carlos's Habsburg predecessors had arranged marriages between cousin and cousin, and uncle and niece. Carlos's father Philip IV had married his niece, Mariana of Austria. Philip's own father had married his second cousin, while Mariana's parents were first cousins. Carlos II was born in 1661, but astonishingly there had not been any new blood in the Habsburg family tree since 1550.

As a result, Carlos's family tree was a very unusual one in many ways, not the least of which was that it actually looked like a tree (if you think about it, this is a very bad sign). Most people have 32 great-great-great-grandparents, but Carlos had just 14, because he was related to the same handful of antecedents via a number of different genealogical routes. In one example, Carlos's great-great-great grandmother Joanna of Castile also happened to be his great-great-great-great grandmother, and his great-great-great-great-great grandmother. In fact, to be strictly accurate, Joanna of Castile was two of Carlos's 16 great-great-great grandmothers, six of his 32 great-great-great-great grandmothers, and six of his 64 great-great-great-great-great grandmothers. As if this were not bad enough, Joanna of Castile was known as 'Joanna the Mad' (as described in Chapter Six), and she may have been the source of some of Carlos's inherited frailties.

Despite his many disadvantages, Carlos was of course a king, and so marriage was inevitable. His bride was the French princess Marie Louise of Orléans, who was understandably distraught at the prospect. Not only was she required to marry the unappealing Carlos, but she was treated with barely concealed hostility at the Spanish court, where her servants were accused of plotting, and her nurse was physically tortured during an interrogation. The couple tried for ten years to produce an heir, but without success, probably because Carlos was infertile and possibly also impotent. Marie Louise became increasingly overweight, and died in 1689 after a nasty fall from her horse.

Carlos was said to be heartbroken, but there was still no heir, and so within three months he had remarried, this time to Maria Ana of Neuberg. However this new union was no more successful in conceiving an heir, and Carlos's health was quickly deteriorating. By the age of 35, Carlos was completely bald, senile, lame, and had lost most of his teeth. For years he had seemed to be on the brink of death, and yet somehow survived. Eventually, at the age of 39, he succumbed. After Carlos's death, his failure to produce an heir led to the 11-year War of Spanish Succession.

What was the Popish Plot?

Between 1678 and 1681, England was increasingly gripped by hysteria over the Popish Plot, a Catholic conspiracy which intended to murder King Charles II, terrorise innocent Protestants, and blow up the Houses of Parliament. Respectable Londoners began arming themselves every time they left the house, while women bought 'silk armour' for protection. Catholics were driven out of London, and many of the conspirators were arrested and charged, with at least 15 being brutally executed for their crimes. It was a major public panic, which is somewhat surprising given that there was actually no credible evidence for a conspiracy of any kind.

The man at the centre of the madness was Titus Oates, who was already known to be a liar and perjurer even before he began making these wild accusations. He had been expelled from Merchant Taylor's School and Westminster for sodomy, and sent down from Cambridge University for not paying a tailor's bill. He then became the vicar of Bobbing, in Sussex, but was soon dismissed for drunkenness, stealing, and sodomy again. He then tried to have a young schoolmaster sacked, by accusing him of sexually abusing the boys in his care, but Oates's story was simply not credible, and the locals were outraged by his perjury. After further misadventures, Oates was taken in by Jesuit groups in Spain and France, but when he returned to England for some reason he turned on the Jesuits. With his friend Israel Tonge, an eccentric priest, he began concocting claims that the Jesuits, a Catholic sect, were plotting to assassinate King Charles II.

The plot was first brought to the king's attention by Christopher Kirkby, who accosted Charles while he was walking in St James's Park. Charles disregarded the warning, and then ignored the story a second time when it was brought to him by Tonge himself. However, Charles did make the mistake of asking the Earl of Danby to look into the matter, and the reason this was a mistake was that Danby so was hostile to Catholics of any stripe that he was willing to believe, or claim, almost anything that would damage them. Danby took Oates seriously, and by September 1678 Oates was being interrogated by the King's Council, where he made a whole raft of accusations, implicating a total of more than 500 Jesuits, Benedictines, Dominicans and other Catholics who were in on the plot. The allegations were preposterous, but one of them hit the mark. One of the men Oates accused was Edward Coleman, secretary to the Duchess of York, and investigations found that he had been corresponding with a French Jesuit. This 'proof' was enough for Danby to grant Oates extraordinary powers, as he was given a retinue of soldiers, and began rounding up known Jesuits.

At this point, the story took a mysterious turn, when the Anglican magistrate Sir Edmund Godfrey was found dead in a ditch, having apparently been killed by his own sword. Godfrey had been involved in Oates's investigation, and so the conspiracy theorists were adamant that he had been murdered by Jesuits, to keep him quiet. King Charles was forced to summon Parliament, to address the growing hysteria. Perhaps as many as 80 leading Catholics were arrested and imprisoned, with some being brutally executed, despite the flimsy evidence. Edward Coleman was hanged, castrated, drawn, and quartered, with his stomach being set on fire while he was still alive. Oates meanwhile was granted a Whitehall apartment, and a huge allowance of £1,200 per year.

However, Oates had never succeeded in convincing King Charles II, who recognised that the hysteria around the supposed plot was to some extent intended as an attack on the King's own wife, as well as his brother James, both of whom were Catholics, and therefore had many enemies. By 1681, the public appetite for the brutal executions had waned, and Charles now seized his chance, and had Oates thrown out of his Whitehall apartment. Oates seems to have become completely fearless by this point, as his response was to publicly denounce the king himself, for which he was promptly thrown into prison for defamation. When Charles died in February 1685, his Catholic brother James II acceded to the throne, and he had a score to settle. Oates was publicly pilloried, pelted with eggs, and then stripped, tied to a cart, and whipped from Aldgate to Newgate.

When did it become fashionable to have an anal fistula?

An anal fistula is an unpleasant medical condition in which a kind of tunnel forms between the anal passage and the skin around the anus. It is often caused by an abscess, which gradually fills with pus. As you might imagine, it is a very painful and unpleasant condition, and yet for a brief period in 17th century France, anal fistulas became the height of fashion.

The source of this apparent bout of collective insanity was King Louis XIV, the beloved Sun King, who contracted an anal fistula in 1686, possibly as a result of his predilection for taking frequent, perfumed enemas. He is believed to have had more than 2,000 enemas over the course of his life, and it was not unusual for these to take place in the presence of courtiers. In fact, almost every aspect of Louis's life was put on display, as his enormous palace at Versailles was filled with French nobles, who were required to be present. This unusual method of holding court served a number of purposes. As well as creating a magnificent spectacle of Royal opulence and ceremony, Louis's court at Versailles also meant that he could keep an eye on his nobles at all times, making them entirely dependent upon his largesse, with no time or opportunity to plot or form alliances in their home provinces.

When Louis's anal fistula was diagnosed, he initially tried a poultice, but this treatment was unsuccessful. He now summoned other anal fistula sufferers from the surrounding countryside, to be used them as guinea pigs, who would try a range of experimental treatments, to see if any of them worked. However, most of the treatments tried at this stage seem to have consisted of bathing in the mineral-rich waters of various spas, which predictably had little effect.

The next option was surgery, although as this was an age before anaesthetics, Louis was unsurprisingly reluctant. To ensure his own safety, he arranged for a number of his guinea pigs to have the surgery first, so that the surgeon could practise. The surgeon in question, the celebrated Parisian Charles-Francois Félix, even designed a brand new surgical tool to carry out the procedure, a 'royally curved' scalpel. In the course of practice, a number of the guinea pigs died, but eventually the surgeon was confident that he knew what he was doing. The Sun King's operation went ahead, in the presence of numerous observers, naturally, and thankfully for all concerned, it was a success. According to the king's secretary, Louis never flinched or made a sound, although I leave it to you to decide how plausible this account is. The surgeon was given piles of money, a noble title, and a country estate as payment, in what is believed to have been the highest medical fee in history.

One of the oddest things about this story is what happened next. As Louis recovered, as many as thirty courtiers came forward, claiming that they too were suffering from an anal fistula, and begging the surgeon to carry out the operation on them. They paraded around the Palace of Versailles, with their buttocks bandaged, claiming to share the king's pain. The only problem was that when the doctor inspected them, in every case he found there was nothing wrong with them. It seems that, in their desperation to build some kind of connection with the king, these courtiers were prepared to go to any lengths, including having their anus cut open. A more productive consequence of Louis's operation was that it raised the status of surgery and medicine in France, and inspired Louis and the court to take a keen interest in the subject.

There is one other bizarre aspect to the story of Louis's anal fistula. According to the 18th century diarist, the Marquise de Créquy, Louis's anal fistula inspired his court composer Jean-Baptiste Lully to write a song expressing the nation's hope that the king would recover. The song was called 'Dieu Sauve le Roi', which means 'God Save the King', and in fact the tune of 'Dieu Sauve le Roi' seems to be exactly the same as that of the British national anthem, which was first published in 1744, more than fifty years after Louis's affliction and Lully's composition. If the Marquise is to be believed, Lully's song was plagiarised by the British, possibly by George Frideric Handel, and presented to either George I or George II sometime in the mid-18th century, which would meant that Britain's national anthem 'God Save the King/Queen' is essentially a song about a French king's bottom.

Which king had himself tortured for fun?

For someone who was born to be king, Christian VII of Denmark was dealt a surprisingly unfortunate hand in life. His mother died when he was just two, and his father Frederick V remarried, to the forceful Juliana of Brunswick-Wolffenbüttel, who then gave birth to a son who was disabled. This meant that Christian, as the elder son, effectively stood in the way of his half-brother becoming king. Juliana's consequent resentment of Christian, along with Frederick's descent into alcoholism, might explain why Christian was put in the care of a sadistic, brutal tutor called Detlev Reventlow, who beat him savagely, on occasions leaving the young prince writhing on the floor, and foaming at the mouth.

Unsurprisingly, Christian became a nervous, insecure boy, who soon began to display signs of madness. He suffered from paranoia and hallucinations, and started to self-harm; he is thought today to have suffered from schizophrenia. When courtiers bowed to him, he would leapfrog over them, or slap them in the face. He masturbated with an alarming frequency, and became obsessed with the idea of being tough and manly, perhaps because he was by nature short and frail. He would roam the streets of Copenhagen, attacking passers-by with his medieval spiked club.

When King Frederick died, Christian became the ruler of Denmark and Norway, at the age of just 16. He was soon married, to Caroline Mathilda, the 15 year old daughter of Britain's mad king George III. The pair failed to hit it off, and Caroline had a miserable introduction to Denmark, as she was banned from bringing over any of her ladies-in-waiting, treated with hostility by Juliana (perhaps out of fear that she might produce an heir), and exposed to an anarchic, sleazy court. Christian largely ignored Caroline Mathilda, publicly announcing that it was 'unfashionable to love one's wife'. Instead, he spent his time rampaging around Copenhagen, trashing shops and brothels, and fighting with the city watchmen. He would often return home in the morning with cuts, bruises, and black eyes.

It was in 1767 that Christian first met an intelligent young doctor named Johann Friedrich Struensée, who soon became his personal physician. In just four years, Struensée quickly rose to political power, becoming effectively the sole ruler of Denmark and Norway, while Christian was by now completely incapable. Struensée also took over Christian's marital duties, openly conducting an affair with Caroline Mathilda, which proved to be his downfall.

Over the course of little more than a year, Struensée implemented a staggering programme of reforms, issuing more than 1,000 'royal' proclamations, at a rate of more than 3 a day. Struensée was inspired by the modern ideas of the Enlightenment, and his reforms were designed to prevent corruption and cronyism, to ensure competent government administration, and remove censorship of the press. However, Struensée was politically naïve, and soon made a great number of enemies, who took the opportunity to openly condemn him in the newly free, uncensored press.

The Danish public were not particularly concerned by Struensée's administrative reforms, but they were outraged by his affair with the queen, and by his treatment of Christian, whose popularity remained largely undimmed. When Caroline Mathilda gave birth to a daughter, Louise Augusta, who bore a striking resemblance to Struensée, public anger erupted into riots. Juliana soon arranged for Struensée to be charged with *lese-majesté*, which means 'violating the dignity of the king'. Juliana was said to have watched with pleasure as

Struensée had his right hand cut off, before being broken on a rack, beheaded, and quartered.

Meanwhile, King Christian's mental state had continued to deteriorate. He suffered from hallucinations, and ranted incoherently. He bashed his head against the wall repeatedly, until he drew blood. He had become fascinated by pain, burning his own flesh, and rubbing salt into the wounds. He asked a male lover, Conrad Holcke, to stretch him on the rack, and whip him until his back bled. Christian continued to reign in name only, while his relatives took charge. He lived like this for a further 36 years, occasionally seen pacing in his rooms, or pulling faces at the windows, before dying of a brain aneurysm in 1808, at the age of 59.

Who was the first and only Emperor of the United States of America?

The answer is Joshua Abraham Norton, an English-born businessman who arrived in America in 1849, at the age of about thirty. Norton's family had made some money in South Africa, and after inheriting his father's estate, Norton began to build a fortune of his own, by trading in real estate in San Francisco. He was soon worth $250,000, a very considerable sum for the time. However, his fortunes changed when he attempted to capitalise on a shortage of imported rice, which had caused the price to rocket from four cents per pound to thirty-six cents. Norton quickly invested $25,000 in a shipment of 200,000 pounds of rice en route from Peru, paying the equivalent of 12.5 cents per pound. However, by the time the boat arrived, a number of other shipments had docked, and the price had slumped to three cents per pound. Norton tried to get out of the contract, but the ensuing litigation bankrupted him. In 1858, he left the city, furious at what he perceived as the failings of the legal system.

When he reappeared in 1859, it seemed that Norton's bankruptcy had tipped his mental state into madness, or at least extreme eccentricity. He returned to San Francisco from his self-imposed exile, and issued an announcement declaring, 'At the peremptory request and desire of a large majority of the citizens of the United States, I, Joshua Norton, declare and proclaim myself Emperor of these United States.' He would later add 'Protector of Mexico' to his self-appointed title. Over the next twenty-one years, he issued a series of royal decrees, including orders for the US Congress to be dissolved, and then when this was ignored, for the US Army to disband Congress by force. Unsurprisingly, Norton's instructions were not taken seriously, and he was ignored.

However, although the US government had no interest in the upstart Emperor, the people of San Francisco soon began to take a different view. San Franciscan newspapers began printing his decrees, and he gained the attention of a reporter named Samuel Clemens, who would later find fame under the pen name Mark Twain, and would base the character of The King in his book 'Adventures of Huckleberry Finn' on Norton. Emperor Norton became something of a celebrity in the city, as he would parade through the streets wearing a garish blue military uniform with gold epaulettes, which had been donated to him by the local US Army post, and an elaborate hat decorated with a peacock feather and a rosette. He would eat for free in the finest restaurants, which would proudly display a brass plaque declaring that their establishment was 'by Appointment to his Imperial Majesty, Emperor Norton I of the United States'. Amazingly, after putting up a plaque, restaurants found that their business would significantly increase. Theatres would routinely reserve balcony seats for the Emperor on opening nights, free of charge, naturally, and policemen would salute him as he passed, humouring him as he conducted inspections their uniforms, and pointed out cracks in the sidewalk. On the rare occasions when Norton did deign to actually pay for anything, the penniless Emperor would do so using his Imperial currency, pieces of paper featuring his own hand-drawn image. He also sold Imperial bonds to tourists, offering a 7% interest rate, which was of course never paid.

Most of Norton's early decrees were simply concerned with his desire for power and recognition, but they gradually became more interesting. He protested against the execution of abolitionist John Brown, an issue which would play a significant role in the conflict leading up to the onset of the American Civil War. He ordered the building of a bridge between San Francisco and Oakland, between the exact points where the Bay Bridge would eventually be built, albeit many years after Norton's death, and completely irrespective of his influence. Norton advocated religious tolerance, and lobbied for the formation of a League of Nations, many decades before the idea would come to fruition. He banned the shortening of his home city's name to the vulgar 'Frisco', an interdict which many San Franciscans still observe to this day.

Most famously, he encouraged tolerance towards immigrants, at a time when there was considerable hostility to the city's Chinese community, which had led to appalling scenes of rioting and murder. On one occasion, an angry mob were on their way to the Chinese district, seemingly intent on more violence, when they found their path blocked by Norton, in his full imperial regalia. The Emperor bowed his head, and recited the Lord's Prayer over and over again, until the mob peacefully dispersed.

On January 8, 1880, Norton collapsed in front of Old St. Mary's Church, on his way to a lecture at the California Academy of Sciences. A policeman quickly called for a carriage to take him to hospital, but Norton died before it arrived. The next day, the San Francisco Chronicle published his obituary on the front page, under the headline, 'Le Roi est Mort' (French for 'The King is Dead'). A local businessmen's association paid for a lavish funeral with an impressive rosewood coffin, and as many as 30,000 people lined the streets to pay their respects, at a time when the entire city's population was just 230,000. Writer Isobel Field later wrote of Norton: 'He was a gentle and kindly man, and fortunately found himself in the friendliest and most sentimental city in the world, the idea being "Let him be emperor if he wants to." San Francisco played the game with him.'